Television Network Daytime and Late-Night Programming

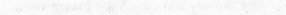

Television Network Daytime and Late-Night Programming, 1959–1989

by
Mitchell E. Shapiro

McFarland & Company, Inc., Publishers
Jefferson, North Carolina, and London

British Library Cataloguing-in-Publication data are available

Library of Congress Cataloguing-in-Publication Data

Shapiro, Mitchell E., 1953–
    Television network daytime and late-night programming, 1959–1989 /
by Mitchell E. Shapiro.
      p. cm.
    Companion volume to: Television network prime-time programming,
1948–1988.
    Includes index.
    ISBN 0-89950-526-0 (lib. bdg. : 50# alk. paper) ∞
    1. Television programs – United States – Chronology. I. Shapiro,
Mitchell E., 1953– Television network prime-time programming.
1948–1988. II. Title.
PN1992.3.U5S535   1990
791.45′0236′0973 – dc20   90-52508
                                                     CIP

Manufactured in the United States of America

McFarland & Company, Inc., Publishers
 Box 611, Jefferson, North Carolina 28640

To my family and friends

Table of Contents

Part Three. Late-Night Programming

Acknowledgments

I would like to thank the faculty, staff and students in the School of Communication at the University of Miami for their support and encouragement.

I would also like to thank the people at McFarland & Company for their assistance and their support with this work.

Finally, I would like to express my most heartfelt thanks to Professor Thomas W. Hoffer of Florida State University for being an inspiration to me in my career. His suggestions and guidance during my graduate studies will always be remembered, and his friendship will always be cherished.

Introduction

This book is designed to be a comprehensive chronicle of network daytime, early morning and late-night television programming. Beginning with September 1959 (or the first programming for each network) and continuing to the fall of 1989, this work provides month-by-month early morning (Monday–Friday, 7:00 a.m. to 9:00 a.m.), daytime (Monday–Friday, 10:00 a.m. to 6:00 p.m.) and late-night (Monday–Friday, 11:00 p.m. to 2:00 a.m.) schedules for all national broadcasting networks; a detailed listing of all network programming moves, including series premieres, cancellations, and time slot moves; and a yearly recap of key programming moves. It also serves as a valuable companion to *Television Network Prime-Time Programming, 1948–1988,* also published by McFarland and Company. Together these two works form the most comprehensive reference set about network television programming.

This book is organized into ten chapters. The first three chapters cover early morning (Monday–Friday, 7:00 a.m. to 9:00 a.m.) programming and include individual month-by-month early morning schedules for each network, followed by a detailed chronological listing of every one of each network's programming moves and a recap of key early morning programming moves for each television season since 1959. (ABC did not begin early morning programming until January 1975.)

The next three chapters cover daytime programming (10:00 a.m. to 6:00 p.m., Monday–Friday) for each of the three major broadcasting networks. Each of these chapters consists of daytime schedules for each network, followed by a detailed chronological listing of that network's programming moves. At the end of each chapter is the recap of key daytime programming moves for each television season since 1959.

The final four chapters cover late-night programming (Monday–Friday, 11:00 p.m. to 2:00 a.m.) for each of the three major broadcasting networks, plus the Fox Broadcasting Company. (Fox is not included in the early morning and daytime sections because as of August 1989 they had not offered any programming during those time periods.) Each of these chapters consists of late-night schedules for each network, followed by a detailed chronological listing of that network's programming moves. At the end of each chapter is the recap of key late-night programming moves for each television season since 1959.

The information contained within this book has been compiled by the author from personal observations. In addition, several sources were used in compiling the program listing information. These sources include *TV Guide*, television listings from Miami *Herald* and Chicago *Tribune*, and *Total Television: A Comprehensive Guide to Programming from 1948 to 1984* by Alex McNeil.

How to Use This Book

The month-by-month program schedules and the detailed listings of all network programming moves are organized by individual network for each different time period. For instance, there is a separate month-by-month schedule and detailed listing for ABC-Daytime (Monday–Friday, 10:00 a.m. to 6:00 p.m.), ABC-Early Morning (Monday–Friday, 7:00 a.m. to 9:00 a.m.), CBS-Early Morning, NBC-Late-Night (Monday–Friday, 11:00 p.m. to 2:00 a.m.), and so on.

On the month-by-month schedules (the chart or grid pages), series are blocked in by time period (all times are based on the Eastern Time zone). Capital letters signify the series' debut. When there is an asterisk at the end of a series block, it signifies that the series was cancelled at that time and no longer appeared on a regular basis.

See "How to Use the Schedule Grids" beginning on page xvii.

The detailed listings of all programming moves (the strictly columnar pages) contain the following information:

Network: the network involved in the specific programming move is shown in the "running head" at the very top of each page.

Date of the action: the month and year (e.g., "8/48") that the specific programming move occurred.

Time: the time in the evening (Eastern Time zone) that the program began.

Title: the specific title of the series.

Length: the length, in minutes, is given in parentheses.

Type: the program type of the series is shown in a two-letter code (after a dash) at the end of each title. The following abbreviations are used:

AD	Adventure	DR	Drama
CA	Comedy Anthology	DS	Discussion
CD	Crime Drama	FI	Film
CO	Comedy-Drama	IF	Information
CR	Courtroom Reenactment	IV	Interview
CV	Comedy Variety	KV	Children's
CY	Comedy	MA	Mystery Anthology
DA	Dramatic Anthology	MD	Medical Drama

MG	Magazine	SC	Situation Comedy
MU	Music	SD	Spy Drama
MV	Musical Variety	SL	Serialized Drama
MY	Mystery	TK	Talk
NA	News Analysis	TS	Testimonial
ND	Newspaper Drama	VS	Various (Umbrella title)
NM	Newsmagazine	VY	Variety
NW	News	WD	War Drama
QU	Quiz/Audience Participation	WE	Western
RA	Crime Anthology		

Action: the specific move that was made by the network. The following moves are included:

d — Debut — when a series first appears on one of the networks' daytime, early morning or late-night schedule

dp — Debut of reruns of a prime-time series on one of the networks' daytime, early morning or late-night schedule

c — Cancelled — when a series last appears on one of the networks' daytime, early morning or late-night schedule

cp — Cancellation of reruns of a prime-time series on one of the networks' daytime, early morning or late-night schedule

m — Moved — when a series is moved to or from a different time slot or to a different network

x — Signifies that a series was occupying a specific time slot on that network's daytime, early morning or late-night schedule prior to September 1959

\# — Used to designate that a series was still occupying that specific time slot at the beginning of the 1989–1990 television season

From/To: when a series was moved (i.e., an "m" appears in the **Action** column); this tells from ("Fr:") where or to ("To:") where and when it was moved. In this column at the right, the following abbreviations are used:

f	Friday
m	Monday
n	Sunday
r	Thursday
s	Saturday
t	Tuesday
w	Wednesday

Several examples, designed to help the reader use and understand the information in the charts detailing all programming moves, are presented below:

This example is from a page headed *"Daytime ABC Schedule"*:

Date	Time	Title (Minutes) — Type	Action	From/To
1/60	1:00	About Faces (30) — QU	d	

In this example, we see that the program involved is *About Faces.* This series consists of 30 minute episodes, and is a quiz/audience participation program, as shown by the "QU" abbreviation at the end of the title. The programming move (the *Action*) is the series debut, represented by the symbol "d." The date of the programming move *(Date)* is January, 1960, and the program occupies the *Time* slot beginning at 1:00 p.m. Eastern Time.

This example is from a page headed *"Daytime CBS Schedule":*

Date	Time	Title (Minutes) — Type	Action	From/To
7/60	10:30	On the Go (30) — VY	c	

In this example the program involved is *On the Go;* it is 30 minutes long, and it is a variety program on the CBS network. It occupied the time slot beginning at 10:30 a.m. Eastern Time, and was cancelled (as signified by the "c" under the *Action* column) in July, 1960.

Note that the two examples so far involved a debut and a cancellation, so there is no information in the *From/To* columns (because there was no "move").

This example is from a page headed *"Daytime ABC Schedule":*

Date	Time	Title (Minutes) — Type	Action	From/To
7/76	3:15	General Hospital (45) — SL	m	Fr:3

In this example, we see that the program involved is *General Hospital,* a 45-minute serialized drama (represented by the abbreviation "SL") on ABC. We can see that the program begins at 3:15 p.m. Eastern Time. We see that there is an "m" under the *Action* column. This means that the programming move involves the series moving to or from this time period, which also means there will be an entry under the *"From/To"* column. In this example, there is a "Fr:3" entry under the *"From/To"* column, which is to be read as "moved from the 3:00 p.m. slot" (and into the 3:15 p.m. slot).

This example is from a page headed *"Daytime NBC Schedule":*

Date	Time	Title (Minutes) — Type	Action	From/To
5/76	10:30	High Rollers (30) — QU	m	To:11-4/78

In this example, the program *High Rollers,* a 30-minute quiz/audience participation program ("QU") on NBC, moved (an "m" under *Action*) to a new time slot. That is, in May 1976 *High Rollers* was moved *out* of its 10:30 a.m. slot and in April 1978 it was moved *into* the 11:00 a.m. slot (i.e., "To: 11-4/78").

This example is from a page headed *"Daytime NBC Schedule"*:

Date	Time	Title (Minutes) — Type	Action	From/To
7/80	10:00	David Letterman Show (90) — TK	m	To:10(60min)

In this example, the *David Letterman Show,* a 90-minute talk show ("TK") on NBC, occupying the time slot beginning at 10:00 a.m. was trimmed to a 60-minute program, but still occupying the time slot beginning at 10:00 a.m. (i.e., "To: 10(60min)").

How to Use
the Schedule Grids

As stated in the previous section, the month-by-month program schedule grids are organized by individual network for each different time period. All early morning (Monday–Friday, 7:00 a.m. to 9:00 a.m.), daytime (10:00 a.m. to 6:00 p.m., Monday–Friday), and late-night (11:00 p.m. to 2:00 a.m., Monday–Friday) television series are blocked in by time period (all times are based on Eastern Standard Time). Capital letters signify the series' debut. An asterisk at the end of a series block signifies that the series was cancelled at that time.

When the title of the series is presented in ordinary capitals and lower-case letters, it signifies that the series was moved into that time slot after airing previously in a different time slot. If one wanted to find out what time slot a series previously occupied, one would simply refer to the monthly listing chart immediately following the program grid. For example, on page 65, one can see that *The Dating Game* was moved into the 4:00 p.m. – 4:30 p.m. time slot in April 1967. To find out where *The Dating Game* aired previously, simply refer to the chronologial chart immediately following the program grid, look up 4/67 which can be found on page 87, and discover that *The Dating Game* was moved from the 11:30 a.m.–12:00 noon slot.

Also in reference to the previous example, one can see that *The Dating Game* occupied the 4:00–4:30 slot (see page 65) until September 1967. Since there is no asterisk listed at that time, it means that *The Dating Game* was then moved into another time slot. To find out where it was moved, simply follow the same procedure described in the previous example — refer to the chart immediately following the program grid, look up 9/67 (page 87), and notice that *The Dating Game* was moved into the 10:00 a.m.–10:30 a.m. slot.

One can also use the program grids to determine exactly what series occupied a specific time slot at any point in time between 1959 and 1989. For example, if one wanted to know what series occupied the 2:00 p.m.–3:00 p.m. slot on ABC's Daytime schedule in April 1978, you would simply turn to the program grid in the ABC Daytime chapter, look up 4/78, look at the 2:00 p.m.–3:00 p.m. slot, and discover that *One Life to Live* occupied that slot at that time (see page 73). If, instead of April 1978, one were interested in what series occupied the 2:00 p.m.–3:00 p.m. slot in January 1979, simply follow the procedure just described. In this case, the series title listed on the grid contains the notation "(cont.)" (see page 75). This signifies that the series that is occupying this slot is the same series listed for this slot on the previous page. In this case we see that it is still *One Life to Live*.

When no series occupies a time slot, the grid is marked with cross-hatching.

Part One
EARLY MORNING PROGRAMMING

ABC Early Morning

January 1975–August 1989

```
          7:00a.m.       7:30a.m.       8:00a.m.       8:30a.m.
1/75  |A.M. AMERICA                                              |
2     |                                                          |
3     |                                                          |
4     |                                                          |
5     |                                                          |
6     |                                                          |
7     |                                                          |
8     |                                                          |
9     |                                                          |
10    |                                                          |
      |                                               *          |
11    |GOOD MORNING AMERICA                                      |
12    |                                                          |
1/76  |                                                          |
2     |                                                          |
3     |                                                          |
4     |                                                          |
5     |                                                          |
6     |                                                          |
7     |                                                          |
8     |                                                          |
9     |                                                          |
10    |                                                          |
11    |                                                          |
12    |                                                          |
1/77  |                                                          |
2     |                                                          |
3     |                                                          |
4     |                                                          |
5     |                                                          |
6     |                                                          |
7     |                                                          |
8     |                                                          |
```

	7:00a.m.	7:30a.m.	8:00a.m.	8:30a.m.
9	Good Morning America (cont.)			
10				
11				
12				
1/78				
2				
3				
4				
5				
6				
7				
8				
9				
10				
11				
12				
1/79				
2				
3				
4				
5				
6				
7				
8				
9				
10				
11				
12				
1/80				
2				
3				
4				
5				

```
           7:00a.m.        7:30a.m.        8:00a.m.        8:30a.m.
 6        |Good Morning America (cont.)                                      |
          |                                                                  |
 7        |                                                                  |
          |                                                                  |
 8        |                                                                  |
          |                                                                  |
 9        |                                                                  |
          |                                                                  |
10        |                                                                  |
          |                                                                  |
11        |                                                                  |
          |                                                                  |
12        |                                                                  |
          |                                                                  |
1/81      |                                                                  |
          |                                                                  |
 2        |                                                                  |
          |                                                                  |
 3        |                                                                  |
          |                                                                  |
 4        |                                                                  |
          |                                                                  |
 5        |                                                                  |
          |                                                                  |
 6        |                                                                  |
          |                                                                  |
 7        |                                                                  |
          |                                                                  |
 8        |                                                                  |
          |                                                                  |
 9        |                                                                  |
          |                                                                  |
10        |                                                                  |
          |                                                                  |
11        |                                                                  |
          |                                                                  |
12        |                                                                  |
          |                                                                  |
1/82      |                                                                  |
          |                                                                  |
 2        |                                                                  |
          |                                                                  |
 3        |                                                                  |
          |                                                                  |
 4        |                                                                  |
          |                                                                  |
 5        |                                                                  |
          |                                                                  |
 6        |                                                                  |
          |                                                                  |
 7        |                                                                  |
          |                                                                  |
 8        |                                                                  |
          |                                                                  |
 9        |                                                                  |
          |                                                                  |
10        |                                                                  |
          |                                                                  |
11        |                                                                  |
          |                                                                  |
12        |                                                                  |
          |                                                                  |
1/83      |                                                                  |
          |                                                                  |
 2        |                                                                  |
          |                                                                  |
```

	7:00a.m.	7:30a.m.	8:00a.m.	8:30a.m.
3	Good Morning America (cont.)			
4				
5				
6				
7				
8				
9				
10				
11				
12				
1/84				
2				
3				
4				
5				
6				
7				
8				
9				
10				
11				
12				
1/85				
2				
3				
4				
5				
6				
7				
8				
9				
10				
11				

	7:00a.m.	7:30a.m.	8:00a.m.	8:30a.m.
12	Good Morning America (cont.)			
1/86				
2				
3				
4				
5				
6				
7				
8				
9				
10				
11				
12				
1/87				
2				
3				
4				
5				
6				
7				
8				
9				
10				
11				
12				
1/88				
2				
3				
4				
5				
6				
7				
8				

	7:00a.m.	7:30a.m.	8:00a.m.	8:30a.m.
9	Good Morning America (cont.)			
10				
11				
12				
1/89				
2				
3				
4				
5				
6				
7				
8				

Early Morning
ABC Program Moves

Date	Time	Title (Minutes) — Type	Action	From/To
1/75	7:00	A.M. America (120) — MG	d	
10/75	7:00	A.M. America (120) — MG	c	
11/75	7:00	Good Morning America (120) — MG	d#	

Early Morning ABC
Programming Moves Summary

1974–75

Series Premieres: A.M. America. *Key Programming Moves:* In January, ABC entered the early morning arena by introducing A.M. AMERICA. Bill Beutel was the host, Stephanie Edwards was the co-host and Peter Jennings anchored the news desk. Similar in structure to NBC's TODAY, A.M. AMERICA had a hard time competing with NBC because of the tradition of TODAY, and because of the smaller number of affiliated stations ABC had compared to NBC (ABC had 183; NBC had 218). In May, ABC decided to go with a single host, and Stephanie Edwards was gone.

1975–76

Series Premieres: Good Morning America. *Key Programming Moves:* In November, ABC replaced A.M. AMERICA with GOOD MORNING AMERICA. Like its predecessor, GOOD MORNING AMERICA was similar in format and structure to NBC's TODAY, though it was lighter in tone. ABC attempted to appeal to a younger, more female audience than TODAY. To this end, the set of GOOD MORNING AMERICA was a homey living room, as opposed to TODAY's newsroom-style set. Also, instead of a journalist, David Hartman, an actor, was named as host. Nancy Dussault was named as the co-host.

1976–77

Key Programming Moves: GOOD MORNING AMERICA was slowly gaining an audience. In April, co-host Nancy Dussault was replaced with Sandy Hill.

1979–80

Key Programming Moves: In early 1980, GOOD MORNING AMERICA overtook NBC's TODAY SHOW in the ratings for the first time ever. At the end of the season, co-host Sandy Hill was replaced with Joan Lunden.

1981–82

Key Programming Moves: By early 1982, GOOD MORNING AMERICA was consistently beating TODAY in the ratings race.

1982–83

Key Programming Moves: GOOD MORNING AMERICA continued to lead the early morning ratings race.

1983–84

Key Programming Moves: GOOD MORNING AMERICA continued to lead the early morning ratings race.

1984–85

Key Programming Moves: GOOD MORNING AMERICA continued to lead the early morning ratings race.

1985–86

Key Programming Moves: GOOD MORNING AMERICA continued to lead the early morning ratings race, but NBC's TODAY SHOW was steadily closing the gap.

1986–87

Key Programming Moves: GOOD MORNING AMERICA and TODAY were in a virtual tie for the early morning lead. David Hartman left GOOD MORNING AMERICA at the end of the season.

1987–88

Key Programming Moves: Charles Gibson replaced David Hartman and joined Joan Lunden as co-host of GOOD MORNING AMERICA.

CBS Early Morning

September 1959–August 1989

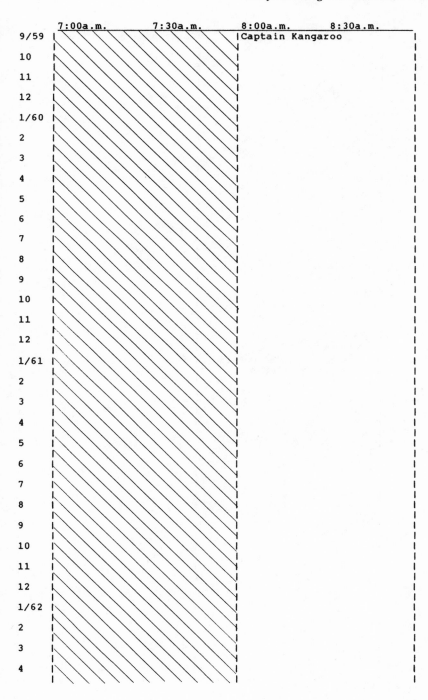

	7:00a.m.	7:30a.m.	8:00a.m.	8:30a.m.
9/59			Captain Kangaroo	
10				
11				
12				
1/60				
2				
3				
4				
5				
6				
7				
8				
9				
10				
11				
12				
1/61				
2				
3				
4				
5				
6				
7				
8				
9				
10				
11				
12				
1/62				
2				
3				
4				

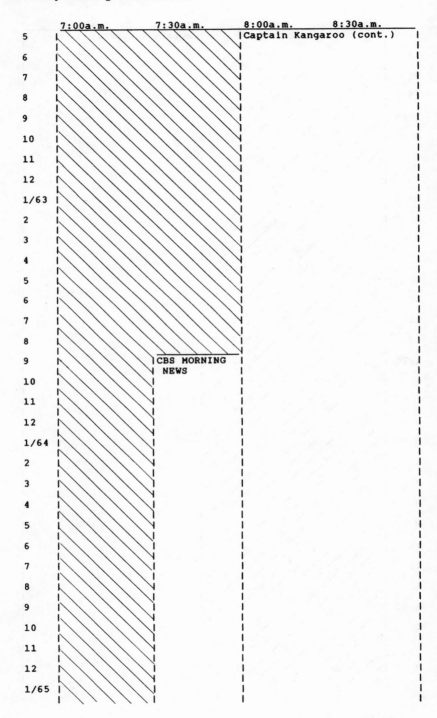

	7:00a.m.	7:30a.m.	8:00a.m.	8:30a.m.
2		CBS Morning News (cont.)	Captain Kangaroo (cont.)	
3				
4				
5				
6				
7				
8				
9				
10				
11				
12				
1/66				
2				
3				
4				
5				
6				
7				
8				
9				
10				
11				
12				
1/67				
2				
3				
4				
5				
6				
7				
8				
9				
10				

	7:00a.m.	7:30a.m.	8:00a.m.	8:30a.m.
11		CBS Morning News (cont.)	Captain Kangaroo (cont.)	
12				
1/68				
2				
3				
4				
5				
6				
7				
8				
9				
10				
11				
12				
1/69				
2				
3	CBS Morning News			
4				
5				
6				
7				
8				
9				
10				
11				
12				
1/70				
2				
3				
4				
5				
6				
7				

	7:00a.m.	7:30a.m.	8:00a.m.	8:30a.m.
8	CBS Morning News (cont.)		Captain Kangaroo (cont.)	
9				
10				
11				
12				
1/71				
2				
3				
4				
5				
6				
7				
8				
9				
10				
11				
12				
1/72				
2				
3				
4				
5				
6				
7				
8				
9				
10				
11				
12				
1/73				
2				
3				
4				

	7:00a.m.	7:30a.m.	8:00a.m.	8:30a.m.
5	CBS Morning News (cont.)		Captain Kangaroo (cont.)	
6				
7				
8				
9				
10				
11				
12				
1/74				
2				
3				
4				
5				
6				
7				
8				
9				
10				
11				
12				
1/75				
2				
3				
4				
5				
6				
7				
8				
9				
10				
11				
12				
1/76				

	7:00a.m.	7:30a.m.	8:00a.m.	8:30a.m.
2	CBS Morning News (cont.)		Captain Kangaroo (cont.)	
3				
4				
5				
6				
7				
8				
9				
10				
11				
12				
1/77				
2				
3				
4				
5				
6				
7				
8				
9				
10				
11				
12				
1/78				
2				
3				
4				
5				
6				
7				
8				
9				
10				

	7:00a.m. 7:30a.m.	8:00a.m. 8:30a.m.
11	CBS Morning News (cont.)	Captain Kangaroo (cont.)
12		
1/79		
2	MORNING PROGRAM	
3		
4		
5		
6		
7		
8		
9		
10		
11		
12		
1/80		
2		
3		
4		
5		
6		
7		
8	*	
9	CBS Morning News	
10		
11		
12		
1/81		
2		
3		
4		
5		
6		
7		

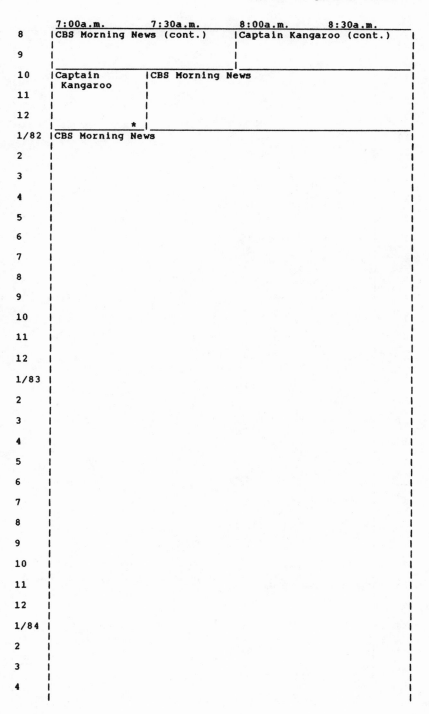

```
         7:00a.m.        7:30a.m.        8:00a.m.        8:30a.m.
  5     |CBS Morning News (cont.)                                      |
        |                                                              |
  6     |                                                              |
        |                                                              |
  7     |                                                              |
        |                                                              |
  8     |                                                              |
        |                                                              |
  9     |                                                              |
        |                                                              |
 10     |                                                              |
        |                                                              |
 11     |                                                              |
        |                                                              |
 12     |                                                              |
        |                                                              |
1/85    |                                                              |
        |                                                              |
  2     |                                                              |
        |                                                              |
  3     |                                                              |
        |                                                              |
  4     |                                                              |
        |                                                              |
  5     |                                                              |
        |                                                              |
  6     |                                                              |
        |                                                              |
  7     |                                                              |
        |                                                              |
  8     |                                                              |
        |                                                              |
  9     |                                                              |
        |                                                              |
 10     |                                                              |
        |                                                              |
 11     |                                                              |
        |                                                              |
 12     |                                                              |
        |                                                              |
1/86    |                                                              |
        |                                                              |
  2     |                                                              |
        |                                                              |
  3     |                                                              |
        |                                                              |
  4     |                                                              |
        |                                                              |
  5     |                                                              |
        |                                                              |
  6     |                                                              |
        |                                                              |
  7     |                                                              |
        |                                                          *   |
  8     |THE MORNING PROGRAM                                            |
        |                                                              |
  9     |                                                              |
        |                                                              |
 10     |                                                              |
        |                                                              |
 11     |                                                              |
        |                                                              |
 12     |                                                              |
        |                                                              |
1/87    |                                                              |
```

```
         7:00a.m.        7:30a.m.        8:00a.m.        8:30a.m.
 2      |The Morning Program (cont.)                            |
 3      |                                                       |
 4      |                                                       |
 5      |                                                       |
 6      |                                                       |
 7      |                                                       |
 8      |                                                       |
 9      |                                                       |
10      |                                                       |
        |                                                      *|
11      |THIS MORNING                                           |
12      |                                                       |
1/88    |                                                       |
 2      |                                                       |
 3      |                                                       |
 4      |                                                       |
 5      |                                                       |
 6      |                                                       |
 7      |                                                       |
 8      |                                                       |
 9      |                                                       |
10      |                                                       |
11      |                                                       |
12      |                                                       |
1/89    |                                                       |
 2      |                                                       |
 3      |                                                       |
 4      |                                                       |
 5      |                                                       |
 6      |                                                       |
 7      |                                                       |
 8      |                                                       |
        |                                                       |
```

Early Morning CBS Program Moves

Date	Time	Title (Minutes) — Type	Action	From/To
9/59	8:00	Captain Kangaroo (60) — KV	x	
9/63	7:30	CBS Morning News (30) — NW	d	
2/69	7:30	CBS Morning News (30) — NW	m	To:7
3/69	7:00	CBS Morning News (60) — NW	m	Fr:7:30
1/79	7:00	CBS Morning News (60) — NW	m	To:7-9/80
2/79	7:00	Morning Program (60) — MG	d	
8/80	7:00	Morning Program (60) — MG	c	
9/80	7:00	CBS Morning News (60) — NW	m	Fr:7-1/79
9/81	7:00	CBS Morning News (60) — NW	m	To:7:30
9/81	8:00	Captain Kangaroo (60) — KV	m	To:7
10/81	7:00	Captain Kangaroo (30) — KV	m	Fr:8
10/81	7:30	CBS Morning News (90) — NW	m	Fr:7
12/81	7:00	Captain Kangaroo (30) — KV	c	
12/81	7:30	CBS Morning News (90) — NW	m	To:7
1/82	7:00	CBS Morning News (120) — NW	c	
7/86	7:00	CBS Morning News (120) — NW	c	
8/86	7:00	Morning Program (120) — MG	d	
10/87	7:00	Morning Program (120) — MG	c	
11/87	7:00	This Morning (120) — MG	d#	

Early Morning CBS Programming Moves Summary

1959-60

Key Programming Moves: CBS continues airing CAPTAIN KANGA-ROO, first aired in 1955. This series, aimed at pre-school aged children, was scheduled in the 8–9 a.m. slot.

1963-64

Series Premieres: CBS Morning News. *Key Programming Moves:* CBS added the CBS MORNING NEWS to its early morning lineup. The CBS MORNING NEWS was a 30-minute straight newscast which aired in the 7:30–8 a.m. slot preceding CAPTAIN KANGAROO. Mike Wallace served as the regular anchorperson.

1965-66

Key Programming Moves: Mike Wallace left the CBS MORNING NEWS at the end of the season.

1966-67

Key Programming Moves: Joseph Benti became the regular news anchorperson on the CBS MORNING NEWS.

1968-69

Key Programming Moves: In March, the CBS MORNING NEWS expanded to one hour, occupying the 7–8 a.m. slot.

1969–70

Key Programming Moves: Joseph Benti was replaced as the regular anchorperson on the CBS MORNING NEWS at the end of the season.

1970–71

Key Programming Moves: John Hart took over as the regular news anchor on the CBS MORNING NEWS.

1972–73

Key Programming Moves: At the end of the season, CBS replaced John Hart as the regular anchorperson on the CBS MORNING NEWS.

1973–74

Key Programming Moves: CBS decided to modify the format of the CBS MORNING NEWS by replacing the single anchorperson with two news anchors. Hughes Rudd and Sally Quinn were selected to be co-anchors for the new CBS MORNING NEWS. In February, CBS replaced Quinn with Bruce Morton, and had Morton anchored in Washington, D.C. while Rudd remained in New York.

1976–77

Key Programming Moves: Hughes Rudd and Bruce Morton were replaced as co-anchors on the CBS MORNING NEWS at the end of the season.

1977–78

Key Programming Moves: Richard Threlkeld and Lesley Stahl were appointed co-anchors of the CBS MORNING NEWS. Former co-anchor Hughes Rudd assumed the role of commentator on the broadcast.

1978–79

Series Premieres: The Morning Program. *Key Programming Moves:* CBS revamped its early morning lineup. In February they replaced the CBS MORNING NEWS with THE MORNING PROGRAM (actually titled MONDAY MORNING, TUESDAY MORNING, WEDNESDAY MORNING, and so on). The new program was done in the magazine format instead of a straight newscast though it was still more news than either TODAY or GOOD MORNING AMERICA. Bob Schieffer was the anchorperson, and Charles Kuralt was "on the road" as a regular contributor.

1979–80

Key Programming Moves: At the end of the season, THE MORNING PROGRAM was cancelled.

1980–81

Key Programming Moves: CBS resurrected the CBS MORNING NEWS to replace the defunct MORNING PROGRAM at the beginning of the season. Charles Kuralt was named anchor of the revamped program.

1981–82

Key Programming Moves: CBS expanded the CBS MORNING NEWS to 90 minutes and moved it into the 7:30–9 a.m. slot. Charles Kuralt continued as anchor, but he was joined by Diane Sawyer. CAPTAIN KANGAROO was cut back to 30 minutes and moved back to 7:00 a.m. In December, after nearly 27 years, CAPTAIN KANGAROO was removed from CBS' daytime schedule. Also in December, the CBS MORNING NEWS expanded again, this time to two hours (7–9 a.m.). In March, Charles Kuralt was replaced with Bill Kurtis. For the next two years the CBS MORNING NEWS would be co-anchored by Kurtis and Diane Sawyer.

1982–83

Key Programming Moves: In August, the CBS MORNING NEWS moved ahead of NBC's TODAY SHOW for second place in the early morning ratings for the first time.

1983–84

Key Programming Moves: CBS continued to gain ground on NBC and fought for second place in the early morning ratings race. Diane Sawyer left the CBS MORNING NEWS at the end of the season in order to join the staff of 60 MINUTES.

1984–85

Key Programming Moves: Phyllis George joined Bill Kurtis as co-host of the CBS MORNING NEWS. The ratings for the CBS MORNING NEWS began a steady decline. In March, Bill Kurtis left the program in order to return to his former position as a news anchor in Chicago. He was replaced by Bob Schieffer.

1985–86

Series Premieres: The Morning Program. *Key Programming Moves:* CBS replaced Bob Schieffer and Phyllis George with Forrest Sawyer and Maria Shriver. CBS continued to be a distant third in the early morning ratings race. In the Spring of 1986, CBS hired Susan Winston, who helped make ABC's GOOD MORNING AMERICA a success, to change the focus of the CBS MORNING NEWS and to improve its ratings. She was not given enough time to change the situation, and in July the CBS MORNING NEWS was cancelled. The 7–9 a.m. time slot was taken away from the news division and was turned over to the entertainment division of CBS. The resulting program was titled THE MORNING PROGRAM, a two-hour magazine format program, similar to TODAY and GOOD MORNING AMERICA, with Mariette Hartley as host.

1986–87

Key Programming Moves: Unable to make a dent in the ratings of TODAY and GOOD MORNING AMERICA, THE MORNING PROGRAM was cancelled at the end of the season, and the 7–9 a.m. time slot was returned to the news division at CBS.

1987–88

Series Premieres: This Morning. *Key Programming Moves:* THIS MORNING debuted on CBS. This magazine program, similar to TODAY and GOOD MORNING AMERICA, hired Kathleen Sullivan (from GOOD MORNING AMERICA) and Harry Smith to serve as co-hosts.

1988–89

Key Programming Moves: While still in third place, THIS MORNING slowly began to build an audience.

NBC Early Morning

September 1959–August 1989

	7:00a.m.	7:30a.m.	8:00a.m.	8:30a.m.
9/59	Today			
10				
11				
12				
1/60				
2				
3				
4				
5				
6				
7				
8				
9				
10				
11				
12				
1/61				
2				
3				
4				
5				
6				
7				
8				
9				
10				
11				
12				
1/62				
2				
3				
4				

	7:00a.m.	7:30a.m.	8:00a.m.	8:30a.m.
5	Today (cont.)			
6				
7				
8				
9				
10				
11				
12				
1/63				
2				
3				
4				
5				
6				
7				
8				
9				
10				
11				
12				
1/64				
2				
3				
4				
5				
6				
7				
8				
9				
10				
11				
12				
1/65				

	7:00a.m.	7:30a.m.	8:00a.m.	8:30a.m.
2	Today (cont.)			
3				
4				
5				
6				
7				
8				
9				
10				
11				
12				
1/66				
2				
3				
4				
5				
6				
7				
8				
9				
10				
11				
12				
1/67				
2				
3				
4				
5				
6				
7				
8				
9				
10				

	7:00a.m.	7:30a.m.	8:00a.m.	8:30a.m.
11	Today (cont.)			
12				
1/68				
2				
3				
4				
5				
6				
7				
8				
9				
10				
11				
12				
1/69				
2				
3				
4				
5				
6				
7				
8				
9				
10				
11				
12				
1/70				
2				
3				
4				
5				
6				
7				

	7:00a.m.	7:30a.m.	8:00a.m.	8:30a.m.
8	Today (cont.)			
9				
10				
11				
12				
1/71				
2				
3				
4				
5				
6				
7				
8				
9				
10				
11				
12				
1/72				
2				
3				
4				
5				
6				
7				
8				
9				
10				
11				
12				
1/73				
2				
3				
4				

	7:00a.m.	7:30a.m.	8:00a.m.	8:30a.m.
5	Today (cont.)			
6				
7				
8				
9				
10				
11				
12				
1/74				
2				
3				
4				
5				
6				
7				
8				
9				
10				
11				
12				
1/75				
2				
3				
4				
5				
6				
7				
8				
9				
10				
11				
12				
1/76				

	7:00a.m.	7:30a.m.	8:00a.m.	8:30a.m.
2	Today (cont.)			
3				
4				
5				
6				
7				
8				
9				
10				
11				
12				
1/77				
2				
3				
4				
5				
6				
7				
8				
9				
10				
11				
12				
1/78				
2				
3				
4				
5				
6				
7				
8				
9				
10				

	7:00a.m.	7:30a.m.	8:00a.m.	8:30a.m.
11	Today (cont.)			
12				
1/79				
2				
3				
4				
5				
6				
7				
8				
9				
10				
11				
12				
1/80				
2				
3				
4				
5				
6				
7				
8				
9				
10				
11				
12				
1/81				
2				
3				
4				
5				
6				
7				

	7:00a.m.	7:30a.m.	8:00a.m.	8:30a.m.
8	Today (cont.)			
9				
10				
11				
12				
1/82				
2				
3				
4				
5				
6				
7				
8				
9				
10				
11				
12				
1/83				
2				
3				
4				
5				
6				
7				
8				
9				
10				
11				
12				
1/84				
2				
3				
4				

	7:00a.m.	7:30a.m.	8:00a.m.	8:30a.m.
5	Today (cont.)			
6				
7				
8				
9				
10				
11				
12				
1/85				
2				
3				
4				
5				
6				
7				
8				
9				
10				
11				
12				
1/86				
2				
3				
4				
5				
6				
7				
8				
9				
10				
11				
12				
1/87				

	7:00a.m.	7:30a.m.	8:00a.m.	8:30a.m.
2	Today (cont.)			
3				
4				
5				
6				
7				
8				
9				
10				
11				
12				
1/88				
2				
3				
4				
5				
6				
7				
8				
9				
10				
11				
12				
1/89				
2				
3				
4				
5				
6				
7				
8				

Early Morning
NBC Program Moves

Date	Time	Title (Minutes) — Type	Action	From/To
9/59	7:00	Today (120) — MG	x#	

Early Morning NBC
Programming Moves Summary

1959–60

Key Programming Moves: NBC continued airing THE TODAY SHOW in the 7–9 a.m. slot. TODAY, which first aired in 1952, was a magazine format program, that is, it consisted of many different stories presented under one common cover. The program was structured into two 60-minute blocks with each block containing news and weather on the hour and half-hour, and different interviews and features in between. During each hour, at 25 minutes after the hour, local stations carrying the program were given five minutes to insert local news. During the 1959–60 season the host of TODAY was Dave Garroway. He was joined by Jack Lescoulie, who was the number two personality on the show and Frank Blair, who read the news. Florence Henderson, and her replacement, Robbin Bain, were the "Today Show Girls."

1960–61

Key Programming Moves: At the beginning of the season, Beryl Pfizer replaced Robbin Bain as the "Today Girl." In May, Anita Colby replaced Pfizer. Major personnel changes occurred in July. Dave Garroway left TODAY and was replaced with John Chancellor. Frank Blair replaced Lescoulie in the number two slot, Edwin Newman replaced Blair as the news reader, and Louise King became the new "Today Girl."

1961–62

Key Programming Moves: The same lineup of personalities continued through the 1961–62 season.

1962–63

Key Programming Moves: At the beginning of the season, the cast of THE TODAY SHOW underwent a major facelift again. Hugh Downs replaced John Chancellor as host, and Jack Lescoulie returned to the number two position. Frank Blair returned to the news desk, where he would continue until March 1975. Actress Maureen O'Sullivan replaced Louise King as the "Today Girl." At the end of the season, Lescoulie left the program for the second time. This time he was not replaced.

1963–64

Key Programming Moves: In April, Barbara Walters joined the cast of TODAY, replacing Maureen O'Sullivan.

1964–65

Key Programming Moves: NBC kept the cast of THE TODAY SHOW intact, and the program continued its dominant position in the early morning ratings race.

1967–68

Key Programming Moves: Former major league baseball player Joe Garagiola joined the cast of THE TODAY SHOW as the number two personality.

1970–71

Key Programming Moves: THE TODAY SHOW underwent a facelift at the end of the season as Hugh Downs departed as host, though the other regulars continued on the program.

1971–72

Key Programming Moves: Frank McGee was named as the new host of THE TODAY SHOW. The other regulars, Frank Blair, Joe Garagiola and Barbara Walters, all continued in their familiar roles.

1973–74

Key Programming Moves: Frank McGee's unexpected death in April forced NBC to make changes in THE TODAY SHOW. Jim Hartz was named to replace McGee as host. Joe Garagiola left the program, and Barbara Walters moved into the number two spot. Frank Blair continued to read the news. In addition, Gene Shalit was added to the cast as an entertainment critic.

1974–75

Key Programming Moves: In March, Frank Blair retired after 22 years on TODAY and was replaced by Lew Wood, who read the news.

1975–76

Key Programming Moves: At the end of the season, NBC made several changes in TODAY (probably, in part, in response to its new competitor, GOOD MORNING AMERICA). Jim Hartz was replaced as host with Tom Brokaw. Barbara Walters left TODAY to sign a huge contract with ABC to become a co-anchor on ABC's evening newscast. Lew Wood was reassigned to reporting the weather. Floyd Kalber was brought in to anchor TODAY's news desk. Gene Shalit continued in his role as entertainment critic, but also assumed other interviewing duties.

1977–78

Key Programming Moves: Jane Pauley was added to the cast of TODAY at the beginning of the season. Lew Wood was replaced by Bob Ryan as weathercaster in March.

1978–79

Key Programming Moves: In July, Floyd Kalber left THE TODAY SHOW, and Tom Brokaw and Jane Pauley assumed the news reading responsibilities in addition to their other TODAY assignments.

1979–80

Key Programming Moves: In March, Bob Ryan, TODAY's weather-caster, was replaced with Willard Scott.

1981–82

Key Programming Moves: In December, Tom Brokaw left TODAY to become anchor of the NBC NIGHTLY NEWS. He was replaced with Bryant Gumbel and Chris Wallace, who served as co-hosts. Jane Pauley, Gene Shalit and Willard Scott continued in their roles. Pauley and Wallace were given the newsreading duties. Chris Wallace left TODAY's staff at the end of the season, leaving Gumbel and Pauley as co-hosts.

1982–83

Key Programming Moves: John Palmer joined THE TODAY SHOW staff as news anchor at the beginning of the season.

1984–85

Key Programming Moves: TODAY started to pick up ground on ABC's GOOD MORNING AMERICA in the ratings.

1985–86

Key Programming Moves: TODAY narrowed the gap between it and GOOD MORNING AMERICA.

1986–87

Key Programming Moves: TODAY and GOOD MORNING AMERICA were in a virtual tie for the early morning lead.

1988–89

Key Programming Moves: John Palmer left THE TODAY SHOW at the end of the season, after anchoring the news desk for seven years. He was replaced with Deborah Norville.

Part Two
DAYTIME PROGRAMMING

ABC Daytime

September 1959–August 1989

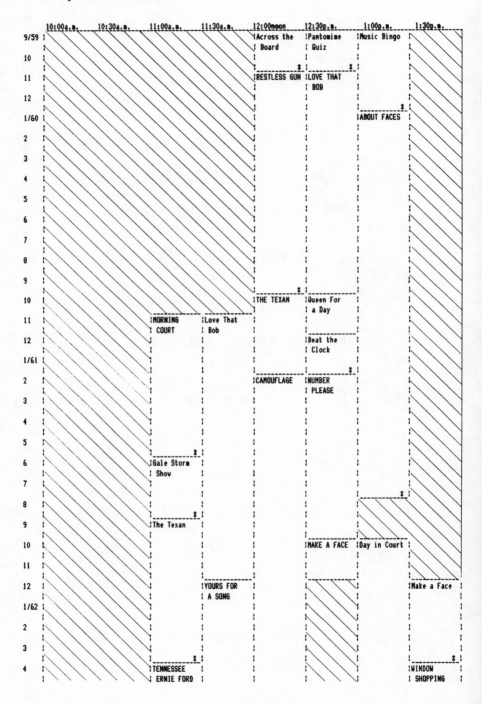

	2:00p.m.	2:30p.m.	3:00p.m.	3:30p.m.	4:00p.m.	4:30p.m.	5:00p.m.	5:30p.m.
9/59	Day in Court	Gale Storm Show	Beat the Clock	Who Do You Trust	American Bandstand			Rin Tin Tin/ MY FRIEND FLICKA
10								
11								
12								
1/60								
2								
3								
4								
5								
6								
7								
8								
9								Rin Tin Tin
10								
11		THE ROAD TO REALITY						
12			Queen For a Day					
1/61								
2								
3								
4		SEVEN KEYS						
5								
6								
7								
8								
9								
10	Number Please							
11								
12								
1/62	JANE WYMAN PRESENTS							
2								
3								
4								

	10:00a.m.	10:30a.m.	11:00a.m.	11:30a.m.	12:00noon	12:30p.m.	1:00p.m.	1:30p.m.
5			Tennessee Ernie Ford (cont.)	Yourd For a Song (cont.)	Camouflage (cont.)		Day in Court (cont.)	Window Shopping (cont.)
6								
7					Jane Wyman Presents		BEST OF GROUCHO	Camouflage
8								
9								
10								FATHER KNOWS BEST
11			Jane Wyman Presents		Tennessee Ernie Ford Show			
12								
1/63								
2								
3	Jane Wyman Presents	Day In Court	Queen For a Day			Father Knows Best	Seven Keys	FILM (to 3:30)
4							GENERAL HOSPITAL	
5				Seven Keys				
6								
7								
8								
9			The Price Is Right					Film (to 2:30)
10								
11								
12								
1/64				THE OBJECT IS	Seven Keys		Tennessee Ernie Ford Show	
2								
3								
4		The Price Is Right	GET THE MESSAGE	Missing Links	Father Knows Best	Tennessee Ernie Ford Show	Film (to 2:30)	
5								
6								
7								
8								
9								
10								
11								
12								
1/65		Father Knows Best	Tennessee Ernie Ford	The Price Is Right	DONNA REED SHOW			

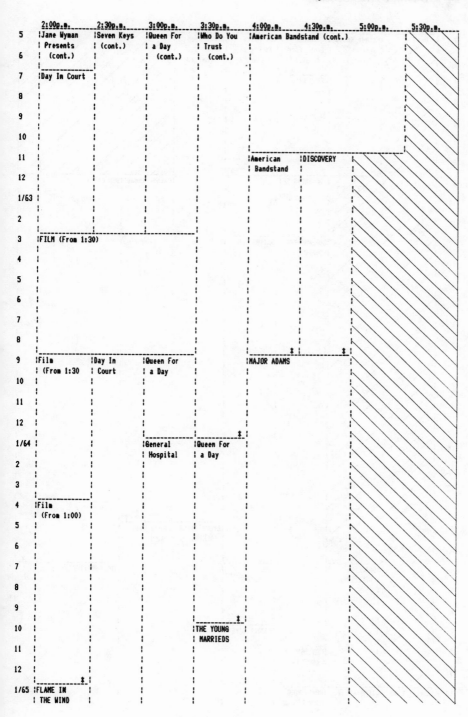

	2:00p.m.	2:30p.m.	3:00p.m.	3:30p.m.	4:00p.m.	4:30p.m.	5:00p.m.	5:30p.m.
5	Jane Wyman	Seven Keys	Queen For	Who Do You	American Bandstand (cont.)			
6	Presents (cont.)	(cont.)	a Day (cont.)	Trust (cont.)				
7	Day In Court							
8								
9								
10								
11					American Bandstand	DISCOVERY		
12								
1/63								
2								
3	FILM (From 1:30)							
4								
5								
6								
7								
8								
9	Film (From 1:30	Day In Court	Queen For a Day		MAJOR ADAMS			
10								
11								
12								
1/64			General Hospital	Queen For a Day				
2								
3								
4	Film (From 1:00)							
5								
6								
7								
8								
9								
10				THE YOUNG MARRIEDS				
11								
12								
1/65	FLAME IN THE WIND							

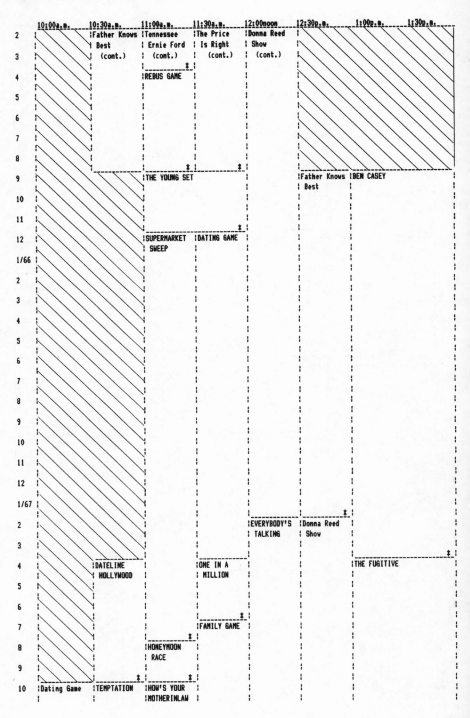

	2:00p.m.	2:30p.m.	3:00p.m.	3:30p.m.	4:00p.m.	4:30p.m.	5:00p.m.	5:30p.m.
2	Flame In the Wind (cont.)	Day In Court (cont.)	General Hospital (cont.)	Young Marrieds (cont.)	Major Adams (cont.)			
3								
4								
5								
6								
7	WHERE THE ACTION IS	Flame In the Wind						
8								
9	THE NURSES				NEVER TOO YOUNG	Where the Action Is		
10								
11								
12								
1/66								
2								
3								
4	CONFIDENTIAL FOR WOMEN			The Nurses				
5								
6								
7								
8	NEWLYWED GAME							
9					DARK SHADOWS			
10								
11								
12								
1/67		DREAM GIRL OF 1967						
2								
3								
4				Dark Shadows	Dating Game			
5								
6								
7								
8								
9								
10								

	10:00a.m.	10:30a.m.	11:00a.m.	11:30a.m.	12:00noon	12:30p.m.	1:00p.m.	1:30p.m.
11	Dating Game (cont.)	Temptation (cont.)	MotherInLaw (cont.)	Family Game (cont.)	Everybody's Talking	Donna Reed Show	The Fugitive (cont.)	
12		Family Game	Temptation	How's Your Mother-In-Law	(cont.)	(cont.)		
1/68		Donna Reed Show			BEWITCHED	TREASURE ISLE		
2								
3		DICK CAVETT SHOW						
4							DREAM HOUSE	WEDDING PARTY
5								
6								
7								
8								IT'S HAPPENING
9								
10								
11								FUNNY YOU SHOULD ASK
12								
1/69						Funny You Should Ask		Let's Make a Deal
2								
3								
4								
5								
6								
7						THAT GIRL		
8								
9								
10								
11								
12								
1/70							ALL MY CHILDREN	
2								
3								
4			Bewitched	That Girl	THE BEST OF EVERYTHING	A WORLD APART		
5								
6								
7								

	2:00p.m.	2:30p.m.	3:00p.m.	3:30p.m.	4:00p.m.	4:30p.m.	5:00p.m.	5:30p.m.
11	Newlywed Game (cont.)	Dream Girl (cont.)	General Hospital (cont.)	Dark Shadows (cont.)				
12								
1/68		BABY GAME						
2								
3								
4								
5								
6								
7								
8		Dating Game		ONE LIFE TO LIVE	Dark Shadows			
9								
10								
11								
12								
1/69								
2								
3								
4								
5								
6								
7								
8								
9								
10								
11								
12								
1/70								
2								
3								
4								
5								
6								
7								

	10:00a.m.	10:30a.m.	11:00a.m.	11:30a.m.	12:00noon	12:30p.m.	1:00p.m.	1:30p.m.
8			Bewitched	That Girl	The Best of	A World	All My	Let's Make
			(cont.)	(cont.)	Everything	Apart	Children	a Deal
9					(cont.)	(cont.)	(cont.)	(cont.)
10					Bewitched			
11								
12								
1/71								
2								
3								
4								
5								
6								
7						LOVE		
8						AMERICAN		
						STYLE		
9						Password		
10								
11								
12								
1/72								
2								
3				Bewitched	Password	SPLIT		
						SECOND		
4								
5								
6								
7								
8								
9								
10								
11								
12								
1/73								
2								
3				Love				
				American				
4				Style				

	2:00p.m.	2:30p.m.	3:00p.m.	3:30p.m.	4:00p.m.	4:30p.m.	5:00p.m.	5:30p.m.
8	Newlywed Game (cont.)	Dating Game (cont.)	General Hospital (cont.)	One Life To Live (cont.)	Dark Shadows (cont.)			
9								
10								
11								
12								
1/71								
2								
3								
4					Password			
5								
6								
7								
8								
9					Love American Style			
10								
11								
12								
1/72								
2								
3								
4								
5								
6								
7								
8								
9								
10								
11								
12								
1/73								
2								
3								
4								

	10:00a.m.	10:30a.m.	11:00a.m.	11:30a.m.	12:00noon	12:30p.m.	1:00p.m.	1:30p.m.
5			Love	Bewitched	Password	Split	All My	Let's Make
			American	(cont.)	(cont.)	Second	Children	a Deal
6			Style			(cont.)	(cont.)	(cont.)
			(cont.)					
7				BRADY BUNCH				
8								
9								
10								
11								
12								
1/74								
2								
3								
4								
5			$10,000					
			Pyramid					
6								
7								
8								
9								
10								
11								
12			MONEY MAZE					
1/75								
2								
3								
4				BLANKETY				
				BLANKS				
5								
6								
7				Brady Bunch	SHOWOFFS	All My	RYAN'S HOPE	
						Children		
8								
9				HAPPY DAYS				
10								
11								
12								
1/76					Let's Make			Rhyme and
					a Deal			Reason

	2:00p.m.	2:30p.m.	3:00p.m.	3:30p.m.	4:00p.m.	4:30p.m.	5:00p.m.	5:30p.m.
5	Newlywed Game (cont.)	Dating Game (cont.)	General Hospital	One Life To Live (cont.)				
6			(cont.)	(cont.)				
7		THE GIRL IN MY LIFE						
8								
9								
10								
11								
12								
1/74								
2								
3								
4								
5								
6								
7								
8								
9								
10								
11								
12	$10,000 Pyramid	BIG SHOWDOWN						
1/75								
2								
3								
4								
5								
6								
7		RHYME AND REASON			YOU DON'T SAY			
8								
9								
10								
11								
12					The Edge of Night			
1/76		THE NEIGHBORS						

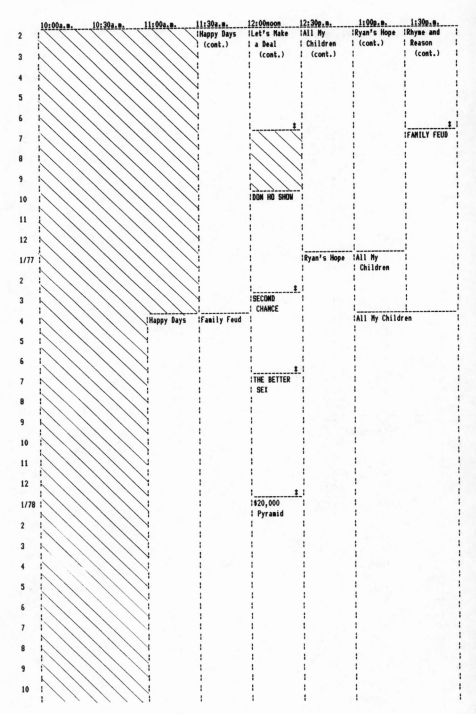

	2:00p.m.	2:30p.m.	3:00p.m.	3:30p.m.	4:00p.m.	4:30p.m.	5:00p.m.	5:30p.m.
2	$10,000	Neighbors	General	One Life	Edge of			
	Pyramid	(cont.)	Hospital	To Live	Night			
3	(cont.)		(cont.)	(cont.)	(cont.)			
4								
5	($20,000	BREAK THE						
	Pyramid)	BANK						
6								
7		One Life To Live		General Hospital				
8								
9								
10								
11								
12								
1/77								
2								
3								
4								
5								
6								
7								
8								
9								
10								
11								
12								
1/78	One Life To Live		General Hospital					
2								
3								
4								
5								
6								
7								
8								
9								
10								

	10:00a.m.	10:30a.m.	11:00a.m.	11:30a.m.	12:00noon	12:30p.m.	1:00p.m.	1:30p.m.
11			Happy Days (cont.)	Family Feud (cont.)	$20,000 Pyramid (cont.)	Ryan's Hope (cont.)	All My Children (cont.)	
12								
1/79								
2								
3								
4			LAVERNE & SHIRLEY					
5								
6								
7								
8								
9								
10								
11								
12								
1/80								
2								
3								
4								
5								
6								
7			LOVE BOAT		Family Feud			
8								
9								
10								
11								
12								
1/81								
2								
3								
4								
5								
6			THREE'S COMAPNY					
7								

	2:00p.m.	2:30p.m.	3:00p.m.	3:30p.m.	4:00p.m.	4:30p.m.	5:00p.m.	5:30p.m.
11	One Life To Live (cont.)		General Hospital (cont.)		Edge of			
12					Night			
1/79					(cont.)			
2								
3								
4								
5								
6								
7								
8								
9								
10								
11								
12								
1/80								
2								
3								
4								
5								
6								
7								
8								
9								
10								
11								
12								
1/81								
2								
3								
4								
5								
6								
7								

	10:00a.m.	10:30a.m.	11:00a.m.	11:30a.m.	12:00noon	12:30p.m.	1:00p.m.	1:30p.m.
8			Three's Company (cont.)		Family Feud (cont.)	Ryan's Hope (cont.)	All My Children (cont.)	
9			Love Boat					
10								
11								
12								
1/82								
2								
3								
4								
5								
6								
7								
8								
9								
10								
11								
12								
1/83								
2								
3								
4								
5								
6								
7			TOO CLOSE FOR COMFORT	LOVING				
8								
9			BENSON					
10								
11								
12								
1/84								
2								
3								
4								

	2:00p.m.	2:30p.m.	3:00p.m.	3:30p.m.	4:00p.m.	4:30p.m.	5:00p.m.	5:30p.m.
8	One Life To Live (cont.)		General Hospital (cont.)		Edge of			
9					Night			
10					(cont.)			
11								
12								
1/82								
2								
3								
4								
5								
6								
7								
8								
9								
10								
11								
12								
1/83								
2								
3								
4								
5								
6								
7								
8								
9								
10								
11								
12								
1/84								
2								
3								
4								

Time columns: 10:00a.m. · 10:30a.m. · 11:00a.m. · 11:30a.m. · 12:00noon · 12:30p.m. · 1:00p.m. · 1:30p.m.

Year/Month	11:00a.m.	11:30a.m.	12:00noon	12:30p.m.	1:00p.m.
5	Benson (cont.)	Loving (cont.)	Family Feud (cont.)	Ryan's Hope (cont.)	All My Children (cont.)
6	LOVE REPORT				
7					
8	CELEBRITY FAMILY FEUD				
9					
10	TRIVIA TRAP	Family Feud	Loving		
11					
12					
1/85					
2					
3					
4	ALL STAR BLITZ				
5					
6	ANGIE	All Star Blitz			
7					
8					
9	THREE'S A CROWD				
10					
11					
12	Ryan's Hope	NEW LOVE AMERICAN STYLE			
1/86					
2					
3					
4	LIFESTYLES OF THE RICH & FAMOUS			Ryan's Hope	
5					
6					
7					
8		DOUBLE TALK			
9	FAME, FORTUNE & ROMANCE				
10					
11					
12					
1/87					

	2:00p.m.	2:30p.m.	3:00p.m.	3:30p.m.	4:00p.m.	4:30p.m.	5:00p.m.	5:30p.m.
5	One Life To Live (cont.)		General Hospital (cont.)		Edge of			
6					Night			
7					(cont.)			
8								
9								
10								
11								
12								
1/85								
2								
3								
4								
5								
6								
7								
8								
9								
10								
11								
12								
1/86								
2								
3								
4								
5								
6								
7								
8								
9								
10								
11								
12								
1/87								

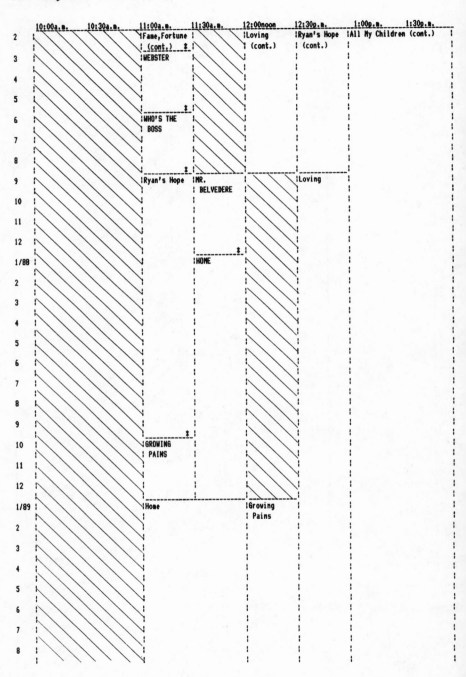

	2:00p.m.	2:30p.m.	3:00p.m.	3:30p.m.	4:00p.m.	4:30p.m.	5:00p.m.	5:30p.m.
2	One Life To Live (cont.)		General Hospital (cont.)					
3								
4								
5								
6								
7								
8								
9								
10								
11								
12								
1/88								
2								
3								
4								
5								
6								
7								
8								
9								
10								
11								
12								
1/89								
2								
3								
4								
5								
6								
7								
8								

Daytime ABC
Program Moves

Date	Time	Title (Minutes) — Type	Action	From/To
9/59	12:00	Across the Board (30) — QU	x	
9/59	12:30	Pantomime Quiz (30) — QU	x	
9/59	1:00	Music Bingo (30) — QU	x	
9/59	2:00	Day in Court (30) — CR	x	
9/59	2:30	Gale Storm Show (30) — SC	x	
9/59	3:00	Beat the Clock (30) — QU	x	
9/59	3:30	Who Do You Trust (30) — QU	x	
9/59	4:00	American Bandstand (90) — MU	x	
9/59	5:30	My Friend Flicka (30) — AD	dp	
9/59	5:30	Rin Tin Tin (30) — WE	x	
10/59	12:00	Across the Board (30) — QU	c	
10/59	12:30	Pantomime Quiz (30) — QU	c	
11/59	12:30	The Restless Gun (30) — WE	dp	
11/59	12:30	Love That Bob (30) — SC	dp	
12/59	1:00	Music Bingo (30) — QU	c	
1/60	1:00	About Faces (30) — QU	d	
8/60	5:30	My Friend Flicka (30) — AD	cp	
9/60	12:00	The Restless Gun (30) — WE	cp	
9/60	12:30	Love That Bob (30) — SC	m	To:11:30-11/60
10/60	12:00	The Texan (30) — WE	dp	
10/60	12:30	Queen for a Day (30) — TS	m	Fr:1:30(n)
10/60	2:30	Gale Storm Show (30) — SC	m	To:11-6/61
11/60	11:00	Morning Court (30) — CR	d	
11/60	11:30	Love That Bob (30) — SC	m	Fr:12:30-9/60
11/60	12:30	Queen for a Day (30) — TS	m	To:3
11/60	2:30	The Road to Reality (30) — SL	d	
11/60	3:00	Beat the Clock (30) — QU	m	To:12:30
12/60	12:30	Beat the Clock (30) — QU	m	Fr:3
12/60	3:00	Queen for a Day (30) — TS	m	Fr:12:30
1/61	12:00	The Texan (30) — WE	m	To:11-9/61
1/61	12:30	Beat the Clock (30) — QU	c	
2/61	12:00	Camouflage (30) — QU	d	
2/61	12:30	Number Please (30) — QU	d	
3/61	2:30	The Road to Reality (30) — SL	c	
4/61	2:30	Seven Keys (30) — QU	d	

Date	Time	Title (Minutes) — Type	Action	From/To
5/61	11:00	Morning Court (30) — CR	c	
6/61	11:00	Gale Storm Show (30) — SC	m	Fr:2:30
7/61	1:00	About Faces (30) — QU	c	
8/61	11:00	Gale Storm Show (30) — SC	cp	
9/61	11:00	The Texan (30) — WE	m	Fr:12-1/61
9/61	12:30	Number Please (30) — QU	m	To:2
9/61	2:00	Day in Court (30) — CR	m	To:1
9/61	5:30	Rin Tin Tin (30) — WE	cp	
10/61	12:30	Make a Face (30) — QU	d	
10/61	1:00	Day in Court (30) — CR	m	Fr:2
10/61	2:00	Number Please (30) — QU	m	Fr:12:30
11/61	11:30	Love That Bob (30) — SC	m	To:11:30-12/62(c)
11/61	12:30	Make a Face (30) — QU	m	To:1:30
12/61	11:30	Yours for a Song (30) — QU	d	
12/61	1:30	Make a Face (30) — QU	m	Fr:12:30
12/61	2:00	Number Please (30) — QU	c	
1/62	2:00	Jane Wyman Presents (30) — DA	dp	
3/62	11:00	The Texan (30) — WE	cp	
3/62	1:30	Make a Face (30) — QU	c	
4/62	11:00	Tennessee Ernie Ford Show (30) — MV	d	
4/62	1:30	Window Shopping (30) — QU	d	
6/62	12:00	Camouflage (30) — QU	m	To:1:30
6/62	1:00	Day in Court (30) — CR	m	To:2
6/62	1:30	Window Shopping (30) — QU	c	
6/62	2:00	Jane Wyman Presents (30) — DA	m	To:12
7/62	12:00	Jane Wyman Presents (30) — DA	m	Fr:2
7/62	1:00	Best of Groucho (30) — QU	dp	
7/62	1:30	Camouflage (30) — QU	m	Fr:12
7/62	2:00	Day in Court (30) — CR	m	Fr:1
9/62	1:30	Camouflage (30) — QU	c	
10/62	11:00	Tennessee Ernie Ford Show (30) — MV	m	To:12
10/62	12:00	Jane Wyman Presents (30) — DA	m	To:11
10/62	1:30	Father Knows Best (30) — SC	dp	
10/62	4:00	American Bandstand (90) — MU	m	To:4(30min)
11/62	11:00	Jane Wyman Presents (30) — DA	m	Fr:12
11/62	12:00	Tennessee Ernie Ford Show (30) — MV	m	Fr:11
11/62	4:00	American Bandstand (30) — MU	m	Fr:4(90min)
11/62	4:30	Discovery (30) — KV	d	
2/63	11:00	Jane Wyman Presents (30) — DA	m	To:10
2/63	1:00	Best of Groucho (30) — QU	cp	
2/63	1:30	Father Knows Best (30) — SC	m	To:12:30
2/63	2:00	Day in Court (30) — CR	m	To:10:30
2/63	2:30	Seven Keys (30) — QU	m	To:1
2/63	3:00	Queen for a Day (30) — TS	m	To:11
3/63	10:00	Jane Wyman Presents (30) — DA	m	Fr:11
3/63	10:30	Day in Court (30) — CR	m	Fr:2
3/63	11:00	Queen for a Day (30) — TS	m	Fr:3

Date	*Time*	*Title (Minutes) — Type*	*Action*	*From/To*
3/63	12:30	Father Knows Best (30) — SC	m	Fr:1:30
3/63	1:00	Seven Keys (30) — QU	m	Fr:2:30
3/63	1:00	Seven Keys (30) — QU	m	To:11:30-5/63
3/63	1:30	Film (120) — FI	d	
4/63	11:30	Yours for a Song (30) — QU	c	
4/63	1:00	General Hospital (30) — SL	d	
5/63	11:30	Seven Keys (30) — QU	m	Fr:1-3/63
8/63	10:00	Jane Wyman Presents (30) — DA	cp	
8/63	10:30	Day in Court (30) — CR	m	To:2:30
8/63	11:00	Queen for a Day (30) — TS	m	To:3
8/63	1:30	Film (120) — FI	m	To:1:30(60min)
8/63	4:00	American Bandstand (30) — MU	c	
8/63	4:30	Discovery (30) — KV	c	
9/63	11:00	The Price Is Right (30) — QU	m	Fr:11(n)
9/63	1:30	Film(60) — FI	m	Fr:1:30(120min)
9/63	2:30	Day in Court (30) — CR	m	Fr:10:30
9/63	3:00	Queen for a Day (30) — TS	m	Fr:11
9/63	4:00	Major Adams (60) — WE	dp	
12/63	11:30	Seven Keys (30) — QU	m	To:12
12/63	12:00	Tennessee Ernie Ford Show (30) — MV	m	To:1
12/63	1:00	General Hospital (30) — SL	m	To:3
12/63	3:00	Queen for a Day (30) — TS	m	To:3:30
12/63	3:30	Who Do You Trust (30) — QU	c	
1/64	11:30	The Object Is (30) — QU	d	
1/64	12:00	Seven Keys (30) — QU	m	Fr:11:30
1/64	1:00	Tennessee Ernie Ford Show (30) — MV	m	Fr:12
1/64	3:00	General Hospital (30) — SL	m	Fr:1
1/64	3:30	Queen for a Day (30) — TS	m	Fr:3
3/64	11:00	The Price Is Right (30) — QU	m	To:10:30
3/64	11:30	The Object Is (30) — QU	c	
3/64	12:00	Seven Keys (30) — QU	c	
3/64	12:30	Father Knows Best (30) — SC	m	To:12
3/64	1:00	Tennessee Ernie Ford Show (30) — MV	m	To:12:30
3/64	1:30	Film (60) — FI	m	To:1
4/64	10:30	The Price Is Right (30) — QU	m	Fr:11
4/64	11:00	Get the Message (30) — QU	d	
4/64	11:30	Missing Links (30) — QU	m	Fr:11:30(n)
4/64	12:00	Father Knows Best (30) — SC	m	Fr:12:30
4/64	12:30	Tennessee Ernie Ford Show (30) — MV	m	Fr:1
4/64	1:00	Film (90) — FI	m	Fr:1:30
9/64	3:30	Queen for a Day (30) — TS	c	
10/64	3:30	The Young Marrieds (30) — SL	d	
12/64	10:30	The Price Is Right (30) — QU	m	To:11:30
12/64	11:00	Get the Message (30) — QU	c	
12/64	11:30	Missing Links (30) — QU	c	
12/64	12:00	Father Knows Best (30) — SC	m	To:10:30

Date	Time	Title (Minutes) — Type	Action	From/To
12/64	12:30	Tennessee Ernie Ford Show (30) — MV	m	To:11
12/64	1:00	Film (90) — FI	c	
1/65	10:30	Father Knows Best (30) — SC	m	Fr:12
1/65	11:00	Tennessee Ernie Ford Show (30) — MV	m	Fr:12:30
1/65	11:30	The Price Is Right (30) — QU	m	Fr:10:30
1/65	12:00	Donna Reed Show (30) — SC	dp	
1/65	2:00	Flame in the Wind (30) — SL	d	
3/65	11:00	Tennessee Ernie Ford Show (30) — MV	c	
4/65	11:00	Rebus Game (30) — QU	d	
6/65	2:00	Flame in the Wind (30) — SL	m	To:2:30
6/65	2:30	Day in Court (30) — CR	c	
7/65	2:00	Where the Action Is (30) — MU	d	
7/65	2:30	Flame in the Wind (30) — SL	m	Fr:2
8/65	10:30	Father Knows Best (30) — SC	m	To:12:30
8/65	11:00	Rebus Game (30) — QU	c	
8/65	11:30	The Price Is Right (30) — QU	c	
8/65	2:00	Where the Action Is (30) — MU	m	To:4:30
8/65	4:00	Major Adams (60) — WE	cp	
9/65	11:00	The Young Set (60) — TK	d	
9/65	12:30	Father Knows Best (30) — SC	m	Fr:10:30
9/65	1:00	Ben Casey (60) — MD	dp	
9/65	2:00	The Nurses (30) — SL	d	
9/65	4:00	Never Too Young (30) — SL	d	
9/65	4:30	Where the Action Is (30) — MU	m	Fr:2
11/65	11:00	The Young Set (60) — TK	c	
12/65	11:00	Supermarket Sweep (30) — QU	d	
12/65	11:30	Dating Game (30) — QU	d	
3/66	2:00	The Nurses (30) — SL	m	To:3:30
3/66	3:30	The Young Marrieds (30) — SL	c	
4/66	2:00	Confidential for Women (30) — DR	d	
4/66	3:30	The Nurses (30) — SL	m	Fr:2
6/66	4:00	Never Too Young (30) — SL	c	
7/66	2:00	Confidential for Women (30) — DR	c	
7/66	4:00	Dark Shadows (30) — SL	d	
8/66	2:00	Newlywed Game (30) — QU	d	
12/66	2:30	Flame in the Wind (30) — SL	c	
1/67	12:00	Donna Reed Show (30) — SC	m	To:12:30
1/67	12:30	Father Knows Best (30) — SC	cp	
1/67	2:30	Dream Girl of 1967 (30) — QU	d	
2/67	12:00	Everybody's Talking (30) — QU	d	
2/67	12:30	Donna Reed Show (30) — SC	m	Fr:12
3/67	11:30	Dating Game (30) — QU	m	To:4
3/67	1:00	Ben Casey (60) — MD	cp	
3/67	3:30	The Nurses (30) — SL	c	
3/67	4:00	Dark Shadows (30) — SL	m	To:3:30
3/67	4:30	Where the Action Is (30) — MU	c	
4/67	10:30	Dateline Hollywood (30) — IV	d	

Date	*Time*	*Title (Minutes)—Type*	*Action*	*From/To*
4/67	11:30	One in a Million (30)—QU	d	
4/67	1:00	The Fugitive (60)—DR	dp	
4/67	3:30	Dark Shadows (30)—SL	m	Fr:4
4/67	4:00	Dating Game (30)—QU	m	Fr:11:30
6/67	11:30	One in a Million (30)—QU	c	
7/67	11:00	Supermarket Sweep (30)—QU	c	
7/67	11:30	Family Game (30)—QU	d	
8/67	11:00	Honeymoon Race (30)—QU	d	
9/67	10:30	Dateline Hollywood (30)—IV	c	
9/67	11:00	Honeymoon Race (30)—QU	c	
9/67	4:00	Dating Game (30)—QU	m	To:10
10/67	10:00	Dating Game (30)—QU	m	Fr:4
10/67	10:30	Temptation (30)—QU	d	
10/67	11:00	How's Your Mother-in-Law (30) —QU	d	
11/67	10:30	Temptation (30)—QU	m	To:11
11/67	11:00	How's Your Mother-in-Law (30) —QU	m	To:11:30
11/67	11:30	Family Game (30)—QU	m	To:10:30
12/67	10:30	Family Game (30)—QU	m	Fr:11:30
12/67	10:30	Family Game (30)—QU	c	
12/67	11:00	Temptation (30)—QU	m	Fr:10:30
12/67	11:30	How's Your Mother-in-Law (30) —QU	m	Fr:11
12/67	12:00	Everybody's Talking (30)—QU	c	
12/67	12:30	Donna Reed Show (30)—SC	m	To:10:30
12/67	2:30	Dream Girl of 1967 (30)—QU	c	
1/68	10:30	Donna Reed Show (30)—SC	m	Fr:12:30
1/68	12:00	Bewitched (30)—SC	dp	
1/68	12:30	Treasure Isle (30)—QU	d	
1/68	2:30	Baby Game (30)—QU	d	
2/68	10:30	Donna Reed Show (30)—SC	c	
2/68	11:00	Temptation (30)—QU	c	
2/68	11:30	How's Your Mother-in-Law (30) —QU	c	
3/68	10:30	Dick Cavett Show (90)—TK	d	
3/68	1:00	The Fugitive (60)—DR	cp	
4/68	1:00	Dream House (30)—QU	d	
4/68	1:30	Wedding Party (30)—QU	d	
7/68	10:00	Dating Game (30)—QU	m	To:2:30
7/68	1:30	Wedding Party (30)—QU	c	
7/68	2:30	Baby Game (30)—QU	c	
7/68	3:30	Dark Shadows (30)—SL	m	To:4
8/68	1:30	It's Happening (30)—MU	d	
8/68	2:30	Dating Game (30)—QU	m	Fr:10
8/68	3:30	One Life to Live (30)—SL	d	
8/68	4:00	Dark Shadows (30)—SL	m	Fr:3:30
10/68	1:30	It's Happening (30)—MU	c	
11/68	1:30	Funny You Should Ask (30)—QU	d	
12/68	12:30	Treasure Isle (30)—QU	c	

Date	Time	Title (Minutes) — Type	Action	From/To
12/68	1:30	Funny You Should Ask (30) — QU	m	To:12:30
1/69	10:30	Dick Cavett Show (90) — TK	c	
1/69	12:30	Funny You Should Ask (30) — QU	m	Fr:1:30
1/69	1:30	Let's Make a Deal (30) — QU	m	Fr:1:30(n)
6/69	12:30	Funny You Should Ask (30) — QU	c	
7/69	12:30	That Girl (30) — SC	dp	
12/69	1:00	Dream House (30) — QU	c	
1/70	1:00	All My Children (30) — SL	d	
3/70	12:00	Bewitched (30) — SC	m	To:11
3/70	12:30	That Girl (30) — SC	m	To:11:30
4/70	11:00	Bewitched (30) — SC	m	Fr:12
4/70	11:30	That Girl (30) — SC	m	Fr:12:30
4/70	12:00	Best of Everything (30) — SL	d	
4/70	12:30	A World Apart (30) — SL	d	
9/70	11:00	Bewitched (30) — SC	m	To:12
9/70	12:00	Best of Everything (30) — SL	c	
10/70	12:00	Bewitched (30) — SC	m	Fr:11
3/71	4:00	Dark Shadows (30) — SL	c	
4/71	4:00	Password (30) — QU	m	Fr:2-9/67(c)
6/71	12:30	A World Apart (30) — SL	c	
7/71	12:30	Love American Style (30) — CA	dp	
8/71	12:30	Love American Style (30) — CA	m	To:4
8/71	4:00	Password (30) — QU	m	To:12:30
9/71	12:30	Password (30) — QU	m	Fr:4
9/71	4:00	Love American Style (30) — CA	m	Fr:12:30
2/72	11:30	That Girl (30) — SC	cp	
2/72	12:00	Bewitched (30) — SC	m	To:11:30
2/72	12:30	Password (30) — QU	m	To:12
3/72	11:30	Bewitched (30) — SC	m	Fr:12
3/72	12:00	Password (30) — QU	m	Fr:12:30
3/72	12:30	Split Second (30) — QU	d	
2/73	4:00	Love American Style (30) — CA	m	To:11
3/73	11:00	Love American Style (30) — CA	m	Fr:4
6/73	11:30	Bewitched (30) — SC	cp	
6/73	2:30	Dating Game (30) — QU	c	
7/73	11:30	Brady Bunch (30) — SC	dp	
7/73	2:30	The Girl in My Life (30) — TS	d	
4/74	11:00	Love American Style (30) — CA	cp	
5/74	11:00	$10,000 Pyramid (30) — QU	m	Fr:10:30-3/74(c)
11/74	11:00	$10,000 Pyramid (30) — QU	m	To:2
11/74	2:00	Newlywed Game (30) — QU	c	
11/74	2:30	The Girl in My Life (30) — TS	c	
12/74	11:00	Money Maze (30) — QU	d	
12/74	2:00	$10,000 Pyramid (30) — QU	m	Fr:11
12/74	2:30	Big Showdown (30) — QU	d	
3/75	11:30	Brady Bunch (30) — SC	m	To:11:30-7/75
4/75	11:30	Blankety Blanks (30) — QU	d	
6/75	11:30	Blankety Blanks (30) — QU	c	
6/75	12:00	Password (30) — QU	c	
6/75	12:30	Split Second (30) — QU	c	

Date	Time	Title (Minutes) — Type	Action	From/To
6/75	1:00	All My Children (30) — SL	m	To:12:30
6/75	2:30	Big Showdown (30) — QU	c	
7/75	11:30	Brady Bunch (30) — SC	m	Fr:11:30-3/75
7/75	12:00	Showoffs (30) — QU	d	
7/75	12:30	All My Children (30) — SL	m	Fr:1
7/75	1:00	Ryan's Hope (30) — SL	d	
7/75	2:30	Rhyme and Reason (30) — QU	d	
7/75	4:00	You Don't Say (30) — QU	d	
8/75	11:00	Money Maze (30) — QU	c	
8/75	11:30	Brady Bunch (30) — SC	cp	
9/75	11:30	Happy Days (30) — SC	dp	
11/75	4:00	You Don't Say (30) — QU	c	
12/75	12:00	Showoffs (30) — QU	c	
12/75	1:30	Let's Make a Deal (30) — QU	m	To:12
12/75	2:30	Rhyme and Reason (30) — QU	m	To:1:30
12/75	4:00	Edge of Night (30) — SL	m	Fr:2:30(c)
1/76	12:00	Let's Make a Deal (30) — QU	m	Fr:1:30
1/76	1:30	Rhyme and Reason (30) — QU	m	Fr:2:30
1/76	2:30	The Neighbors (30) — QU	d	
4/76	2:30	The Neighbors (30) — QU	c	
5/76	2:30	Break the Bank (30) — QU	d	
6/76	12:00	Let's Make a Deal (30) — QU	c	
6/76	1:30	Rhyme and Reason (30) — QU	c	
6/76	2:30	Break the Bank (30) — QU	c	
6/76	3:00	General Hospital (30) — SL	m	To:3:15
6/76	3:30	One Life to Live (30) — SL	m	To:2:30
7/76	1:30	Family Feud (30) — QU	d	
7/76	2:30	One Life to Live (45) — SL	m	Fr:3:30
7/76	3:15	General Hospital (45) — SL	m	Fr:3
10/76	12:00	Don Ho Show (30) — VY	d	
12/76	12:30	All My Children (30) — SL	m	To:1
12/76	1:00	Ryan's Hope (30) — SL	m	To:12:30
1/77	12:30	Ryan's Hope (30) — SL	m	Fr:1
1/77	1:00	All My Children (30) — SL	m	Fr:12:30
2/77	12:00	Don Ho Show (30) — VY	c	
3/77	11:30	Happy Days (30) — SC	m	To:11
3/77	12:00	Second Chance (30) — QU	d	
3/77	1:00	All My Children (30) — SL	m	To:1(60min)
3/77	1:30	Family Feud (30) — QU	m	To:11:30
4/77	11:00	Happy Days (30) — SC	m	Fr:11:30
4/77	11:30	Family Feud (30) — QU	m	Fr:1:30
4/77	1:00	All My Children (60) — SL	m#	Fr:1(30min)
6/77	12:00	Second Chance (30) — QU	c	
7/77	12:00	Better Sex (30) — QU	d	
12/77	12:00	Better Sex (30) — QU	c	
12/77	2:00	$20,000 Pyramid (30) — QU	m	To:12
12/77	2:30	One Life to Live (45) — SL	m	To:2
12/77	3:15	General Hospital (45) — SL	m	To:3
1/78	12:00	$20,000 Pyramid (30) — QU	m	Fr:2
1/78	2:00	One Life to Live (60) — SL	m#	Fr:2:30

Date	Time	Title (Minutes) — Type	Action	From/To
1/78	3:00	General Hospital (60) — SL	m#	Fr:3:15
3/79	11:00	Happy Days (30) — SC	cp	
4/79	11:00	Laverne & Shirley (30) — SC	dp	
6/80	11:00	Laverne & Shirley (30) — SC	cp	
6/80	11:30	Family Feud (30) — QU	m	To:12
6/80	12:00	$20,000 Pyramid (30) — QU	m	To:10-9/82(c)
7/80	11:00	Love Boat (60) — CO	dp	
7/80	12:00	Family Feud (30) — QU	m	Fr:11:30
5/81	11:00	Love Boat (60) — CO	m	To:11-9/81
6/81	11:00	Three's Company (60) — SC	dp	
8/81	11:00	Three's Company (60) — SC	cp	
9/81	11:00	Love Boat (60) — CO	m	Fr:11-5/81
6/83	11:00	Love Boat (60) — CO	cp	
7/83	11:00	Too Close for Comfort (30) — SC	dp	
7/83	11:30	Loving (30) — SL	d	
8/83	11:00	Too Close for Comfort (30) — SC	cp	
9/83	11:00	Benson (30) — SC	dp	
5/84	11:00	Benson (30) — SC	cp	
6/84	11:00	Love Report (30) — MG	d	
7/84	11:00	Love Report (30) — MG	c	
8/84	11:00	Celebrity Family Feud (30) — QU	d	
9/84	11:00	Celebrity Family Feud (30) — QU	c	
9/84	11:30	Loving (30) — SL	m	To:12
9/84	12:00	Family Feud (30) — QU	m	To:11:30
10/84	11:00	Trivia Trap (30) — QU	d	
10/84	11:30	Family Feud (30) — QU	m	Fr:12
10/84	12:00	Loving (30) — SL	m	Fr:11:30
3/85	11:00	Trivia Trap (30) — QU	c	
4/85	11:00	All Star Blitz (30) — QU	d	
5/85	11:00	All Star Blitz (30) — QU	m	To:11:30
5/85	11:30	Family Feud (30) — QU	c	
6/85	11:00	Angie (30) — SC	dp	
6/85	11:30	All Star Blitz (30) — QU	m	Fr:11
8/85	11:00	Angie (30) — SC	cp	
8/85	4:00	Edge of Night (30) — SL	c	
9/85	11:00	Three's a Crowd (30) — SC	dp	
11/85	11:00	Three's a Crowd (30) — SC	cp	
11/85	11:30	All Star Blitz (30) — QU	c	
11/85	12:30	Ryan's Hope (30) — SL	m	To:11
12/85	11:00	Ryan's Hope (30) — SL	m	Fr:12:30
12/85	11:30	New Love American Style (30) — CA	d	
3/86	11:00	Ryan's Hope (30) — SL	m	To:12:30
4/86	11:00	Lifestyles of the Rich & Famous (30) — MG	d	
4/86	12:30	Ryan's Hope (30) — SL	m	Fr:11
7/86	11:30	New Love American Style (30) — CA	c	
8/86	11:00	Lifestyles of the Rich & Famous (30) — MG	c	
8/86	11:30	Double Talk (30) — QU	d	
9/86	11:00	Fame, Fortune & Romance (30) — MG	d	

Date	Time	Title (Minutes) — Type	Action	From/To
12/86	11:30	Double Talk (30) — QU	c	
2/87	11:00	Fame, Fortune & Romance (30) — MG	c	
3/87	11:00	Webster (30) — SC	dp	
5/87	11:00	Webster (30) — SC	cp	
6/87	11:00	Who's the Boss (30) — SC	dp	
8/87	11:00	Who's the Boss (30) — SC	cp	
8/87	12:00	Loving (30) — SL	m	To:12:30
8/87	12:30	Ryan's Hope (30) — SL	m	To:11
9/87	11:00	Ryan's Hope (30) — SL	m	Fr:12:30
9/87	11:30	Mr. Belvedere (30) — SC	dp	
9/87	12:30	Loving (30) — SL	m#	Fr:12
12/87	11:30	Mr. Belvedere (30) — SC	cp	
1/88	11:30	Home (30) — IF	d	
9/88	11:00	Ryan's Hope (30) — SL	c	
10/88	11:00	Growing Pains (30) — SC	dp	
12/88	11:00	Growing Pains (30) — SC	m	To:12
12/88	11:30	Home (30) — IF	m	To:11
1/89	11:00	Home (60) — IF	m#	Fr:11:30
1/89	12:00	Growing Pains (30) — SC	m#	Fr:11

Daytime ABC
Programming Moves Summary

1959–60

Series Premieres: About Faces; Love That Bob; My Friend Flicka; The Restless Gun. *Key Programming Moves:* ABC replaced two quiz programs (ACROSS THE BOARD and PANTOMIME QUIZ) with reruns of prime-time series in the 12–1 p.m. slot (THE RESTLESS GUN and LOVE THAT BOB). Reruns of another prime-time series, MY FRIEND FLICKA, were placed in the 5:30–6 p.m. slot, alternating with THE ADVENTURES OF RIN TIN TIN. At the end of the season, MY FRIEND FLICKA was cancelled.

1960–61

Series Premieres: Camouflage; Morning Court; Number Please; The Road to Reality; Seven Keys; The Texan. *Key Programming Moves:* ABC expanded its daytime schedule by airing programming in the 11–12 slot for the first time. ABC introduced MORNING COURT, a companion to its successful afternoon series DAY IN COURT; the new series did not fare too well and was cancelled in May. In December, QUEEN FOR A DAY was picked up from NBC and moved into the 3–3:30 slot. SEVEN KEYS debut in the 2:30–3 slot in April; together with QUEEN FOR A DAY and WHO DO YOU TRUST, which followed SEVEN KEYS, ABC offered a fairly strong 90 minute afternoon block for the next two years. At the end of the season, ABC discontinued programming the 5:30–6 p.m. slot.

1961–62

Series Premieres: The Best of Groucho; Jane Wyman Presents; Make a Face; The Tennessee Ernie Ford Show; Window Shopping; Yours for a Song. *Key Programming Moves:* THE TENNESSEE ERNIE FORD SHOW debuted in April. This light variety series occupied a spot on ABC's daytime schedule until March 1965. CAMOUFLAGE was cancelled at the end of the season. AMERICAN BANDSTAND was cut back to 30 minutes (from its original 90 minutes) at the end of the season.

1962–63

Series Premieres: Discovery; Father Knows Best; General Hospital. *Key Programming Moves:* Reruns of prime-time's FATHER KNOWS BEST began a daytime run on ABC that would last over four years. GENERAL HOSPITAL debuted in April; this soap opera would become a fixture on ABC's daytime schedule, running for over 25 years, and still going strong heading into the 1990s. In the early 1980s, GENERAL HOSPITAL would become the highest rated soap opera on television. AMERICAN BANDSTAND left ABC's daytime schedule at the end of the season; it continued to air on ABC's Saturday schedule for the next 25 years.

1963–64

Series Premieres: Get the Message; Major Adams; The Object Is. *Key Programming Moves:* THE PRICE IS RIGHT was picked up from NBC. It did not perform as well as ABC had hoped, though it did run for two more years. Reruns of the prime-time series WAGON TRAIN began airing in daytime under the title MAJOR ADAMS. In January, GENERAL HOSPITAL was moved to 3:00, where it would air for the next 26 years. SEVEN KEYS was cancelled in March, and QUEEN FOR A DAY was cancelled at the end of the season.

1964–65

Series Premieres: The Donna Reed Show; Flame in the Wind; The Rebus Game; Where the Action Is; The Young Marrieds. *Key Programming Moves:* In January, ABC shuffled its morning lineup, adding reruns of THE DONNA REED SHOW and cancelling two series (GET THE MESSAGE and MISSING LINKS). ABC consolidated its morning block to two hours (10:30–12:30) and ceased programming from 12:30–2 p.m. WHERE THE ACTION IS, a teen-oriented program featuring rock music, debuted in July. Two long-running daytime series were cancelled, DAY IN COURT in June, and THE PRICE IS RIGHT at the end of the season.

1965–66

Series Premieres: Ben Casey; Confidential for Women; The Dating Game; Never Too Young; The Nurses; Supermarket Sweep; The Young Set. *Key Programming Moves:* ABC readjusted its daytime schedule, now offering programming from 11 a.m. until 5 p.m. ABC made a strong push for younger viewers which is reflected in its new series (THE YOUNG SET, THE DATING GAME, NEVER TOO YOUNG, THE NURSES, and reruns of prime-time's BEN CASEY, along with the continuing WHERE THE ACTION IS). Of all their new offerings, only THE DATING GAME became a bona-fide hit series, staying on ABC's daytime schedule until June 1973.

1966–67

Series Premieres: Dark Shadows; Dateline Hollywood; Dream Girl of 1967; Everybody's Talking; The Family Game; The Fugitive; Honeymoon Race; The Newlywed Game; One in a Million. *Key Programming Moves:* ABC attempted to play off the success of THE DATING GAME by introducing THE FAMILY GAME, THE NEWLYWED GAME and DREAM GIRL OF 1967. THE NEWLYWED GAME caught on and became a major hit for ABC. ABC continued to program toward a younger audience and introduced DARK SHADOWS, a soap opera geared toward the younger audience. It caught on and became an important part of ABC's afternoon schedule. FATHER KNOWS BEST was cancelled in January. THE NURSES and WHERE THE ACTION IS were cancelled in March.

1967–68

Series Premieres: The Baby Game; Bewitched; The Dick Cavett Show; Dream House; How's Your Mother-in-Law; Temptation; Treasure Isle; Wedding Party. *Key Programming Moves:* THE DICK CAVETT SHOW, a 90-minute talk program, made its debut in March. It lasted on daytime less than one year and was eventually moved to ABC's late-night schedule. ABC began airing reruns of prime-time's BEWITCHED in January. THE DONNA REED SHOW was cancelled in February.

1968–69

Series Premieres: Funny You Should Ask; It's Happening; One Life to Live; That Girl. *Key Programming Moves:* With the cancellation of

THE DICK CAVETT SHOW in January, ABC ceased airing programming before noon. ONE LIFE TO LIVE debuted in the 3:30–4 p.m. slot, beginning a highly successful run on ABC lasting for over 20 years. THE DATING GAME was moved into the 2:30–3 p.m., slot and DARK SHADOWS was moved into the 4–4:30 p.m. slot. Along with THE NEWLYWED GAME (2–3:30 p.m.) and GENERAL HOSPITAL (3–3:30 p.m.), ABC had a strong, stable afternoon lineup for the first time. In January, LET'S MAKE A DEAL was picked up from NBC; it stayed on ABC's daytime schedule until June 1976.

1969–70

Series Premieres: All My Children; The Best of Everything; A World Apart. *Key Programming Moves:* ALL MY CHILDREN debuted in January. This series became one of ABC's most successful soap operas of all time. It was still going strong at the end of the 1988–89 season. In April, ABC resumed programming the 11–12 hour, though at the end of the season they stopped offering programming from 11–11:30 a.m.

1970–71

Series Premieres: Love American Style. *Key Programming Moves:* PASSWORD was revived by ABC in April. It replaced the cancelled soap opera DARK SHADOWS.

1971–72

Series Premieres: Split Second. *Key Programming Moves:* ABC's daytime schedule remained relatively intact during the 1971–72 season.

1972–73

Series Premieres: The Brady Bunch; The Girl in My Life. *Key Programming Moves:* In March, ABC resumed programming during the 11–11:30 a.m. slot but ceased programming in the 4–4:30 p.m. slot. BEWITCHED and THE DATING GAME were cancelled in June. ABC tried unsuccessful to revive a formula from an old series — THE GIRL IN MY LIFE debuted in July. It was a modern version of QUEEN FOR A DAY. It lasted only a little over a year.

1973-74

Key Programming Moves: THE $10,000 PYRAMID was picked up from CBS in May.

1974-75

Series Premieres: The Big Showdown; Blankety Blanks; Money Maze; Rhyme and Reason; Ryan's Hope; Showoffs; You Don't Say. *Key Programming Moves:* THE NEWLYWED GAME was cancelled in November. PASSWORD and SPLIT SECOND were cancelled in June. RYAN'S HOPE debuted in July. This soap opera lasted until September 1988.

1975-76

Series Premieres: Break the Bank; Family Feud; Happy Days; The Neighbors. *Key Programming Moves:* ABC adjusted its daytime schedule again, this time from 11 a.m.–4 p.m. to 11:30 a.m.–4:30 p.m. Reruns of prime-time's HAPPY DAYS debuted. In December, THE EDGE OF NIGHT was picked up from CBS and placed in the 4–4:30 p.m. slot, where it stayed until its cancellation in August 1985. In May, THE $10,000 PYRAMID became THE $20,000 PYRAMID. LET'S MAKE A DEAL was cancelled in June. FAMILY FEUD debuted in July; this series became one of the most successful daytime quiz programs of all time. Also in July, ONE LIFE TO LIVE and GENERAL HOSPITAL were each expanded to 45 minutes.

1976-77

Series Premieres: The Better Sex; The Don Ho Show; Second Chance. *Key Programming Moves:* In April, ABC resumed programming the 11–11:30 a.m. slot, and ALL MY CHILDREN was expanded to one hour.

1977-78

Key Programming Moves: In January, ONE LIFE TO LIVE and GENERAL HOSPITAL were each expanded to one hour.

1978–79

Series Premieres: Laverne & Shirley. *Key Programming Moves:* HAPPY DAYS was cancelled in March and replaced with reruns of prime-time's LAVERNE & SHIRLEY.

1979–80

Series Premieres: Love Boat. *Key Programming Moves:* ABC's daytime lineup remained relatively stable and was performing well.

1980–81

Series Premieres: Three's Company. *Key Programming Moves:* ABC's daytime lineup remains intact and continues to dominate the ratings.

1981–82

Key Programming Moves: ABC's daytime lineup remained intact and continued to dominate the ratings.

1982–83

Series Premieres: Loving; Too Close for Comfort. *Key Programming Moves:* ABC's daytime lineup remained intact and continued to dominate the ratings. LOVING debuted in July. It became modestly successful for ABC.

1983–84

Series Premieres: Benson; Celebrity Family Feud; The Love Report. *Key Programming Moves:* ABC had trouble finding a winning combination for its 11–12 a.m. slot. Otherwise, ABC's daytime schedule was in very strong shape.

1984–85

Series Premieres: All Star Blitz; Angie; Trivia Trap. *Key Programming Moves:* ABC still had trouble with the 11–12 a.m. slot. FAMILY FEUD was cancelled in May. The EDGE OF NIGHT was cancelled at the end of the season, and ABC did not resume programming in the 4–4:30 p.m. slot.

1985–86

Series Premieres: Double Talk; Lifestyles of the Rich & Famous; The New Love American Style; Three's a Crowd. *Key Programming Moves:* For the third consecutive year, ABC had trouble finding a winning combination in the 11–12 a.m. slot.

1986–87

Series Premieres: Fame, Fortune & Romance; Webster; Who's the Boss. *Key Programming Moves:* For the fourth consecutive year, ABC had trouble finding a winning combination in the 11–12 a.m. slot.

1987–88

Series Premieres: Home; Mr. Belvedere. *Key Programming Moves:* RYAN'S HOPE was cancelled at the end of the season.

1988–89

Series Premieres: Growing Pains. *Key Programming Moves:* In January, HOME was expanded to 60 minutes.

CBS Daytime

September 1959–August 1989

	10:00a.m.	10:30a.m.	11:00a.m.	11:30a.m.	12:00noon	12:30p.m.	1:00p.m.	1:30p.m.
9/59		On the Go	I LOVE LUCY	Top Dollar	A Bright Day	Secret Storm	Search For	Guidng Light	Love of Life	As the World Turns
10							Tomorw			
11				DECEMBER BRIDE						
12										
1/60										
2										
3										
4										
5										
6										
7										
8		VIDEO VILLAGE		CLEAR HORIZON						
9										
10										
11										
12										
1/61										
2										
3										
4	I Love Lucy		DOUBLE EXPOSURE	YOUR SURPRISE PACKAGE						
5										
6										
7										
8										
9										
10	CALENDAR		I Love Lucy							
11										
12										
1/62										
2										
3				Clear Horizon						
4										

	2:00p.m.	2:30p.m.	3:00p.m.	3:30p.m.	4:00p.m.	4:30p.m.	5:00p.m.	5:30p.m.
9/59	For Better Or Worse	Art Linkletter's House Party	Big Payoff	The Verdict Is Yours		The Edge of Night		
10								
11			THE MILLIONAIRE		RED ROWE SHOW			
12								
1/60								
2								
3								
4								
5								
6								
7	FULL CIRCLE							
8								
9								
10								
11								
12								
1/61								
2								
3								
4	FACE THE FACTS							
5								
6								
7								
8								
9								
10	PASSWORD							
11								
12								
1/62								
2								
3								
4								

	10:00a.m.	10:30a.m.	11:00a.m.	11:30a.m.	12:00noon	12:30p.m.		1:00p.m.	1:30p.m.
5	Calendar (cont.)	Video Village (cont.)	I Love Lucy (cont.)	Clear Horizon (cont.)	Bright Day (cont.)	Secret Storm (cont.)	Search For Tomorr (cont.)	Guide Light (cont.)	Love of Life (cont.)	As the World Turns (cont.)
6										
7		I Love Lucy	The Verdict Is Yours	The Edge of Night						
8										
9										
10			REAL MCCOYS							
11										
12				Love That Bob						
1/63										
2										
3										
4										
5										
6										
7										
8										
9										
10										
11										
12										
1/64										
2										
3										
4										
5										
6										
7										
8										
9										
10	Real McCoys		ANDY GRIFFITH SHOW							
11										
12										
1/65										

	2:00p.m.	2:30p.m.	3:00p.m.	3:30p.m.	4:00p.m.	4:30p.m.	5:00p.m.	5:30p.m.
5	Password (cont.)	Art Linkletter's House Party (cont.)	Millionaire (cont.)	The Verdict Is Yours (cont.)		The Edge of Night (cont.)		
6								
7				TO TELL THE TRUTH	Secret Storm			
12						The Edge of Night		
1/63			To Tell the Truth	The Millionaire				
7				The Edge of Night		The Millionaire		

	10:00a.m.	10:30a.m.	11:00a.m.	11:30a.m.	12:00noon	12:30p.m.		1:00p.m.	1:30p.m.
2	Real McCoys (cont.)	I Love Lucy (cont.)	Andy Griffith Show (cont.)	Love That Bob (cont.)		Search For Tomorr (cont)	Guide Light (cont)	Love of Life (cont.)	As the World Turns (cont.)
3									
4									
5									
6									
7									
8		Love That Bob P.D.Q.		DICK VAN DYKE SHOW					
9									
10									
11									
12									
1/66		I Love Lucy							
2									
3									
4									
5									
6									
7									
8									
9									
10	I Love Lucy	BEVERLY HILLBILLIES							
11									
12									
1/67									
2									
3									
4									
5									
6									
7									
8									
9									
10	PETTICOAT JUNCTION								

	2:00p.m.	2:30p.m.	3:00p.m.	3:30p.m.	4:00p.m.	4:30p.m.	5:00p.m.	5:30p.m.
2	Password (cont.)	Art Linkletter's House Party (cont.)	To Tell the Truth (cont.)	The Edge of Night (cont.)	Secret Storm (cont.)			
3								
4								
5								
6								
7								
8								
9								
10								
11								
12								
1/66								
2								
3								
4								
5								
6								
7								
8								
9								
10								
11								
12								
1/67								
2								
3								
4								
5								
6								
7								
8								
9								
10	LOVE IS A MANY SPLENDOR THING							

	10:00a.m.	10:30a.m.	11:00a.m.	11:30a.m.	12:00noon	12:30p.m.	1:00p.m.	1:30p.m.
11	Petticoat	Beverly	Andy	Dick Van		Search	Guide	Love of Life	As the World
12	Junction (cont.)	Hillbillies (cont.)	Griffith Show (cont.)	Dyke Show (cont.)		For Tomorr (cont.)	Light (cont.)	(cont.)	Turns (cont.)
1/68								
2								
3								
4								
5								
6								
7								
8								
9	LUCY SHOW							
10						Search For Tomorrow		
11								
12								
1/69								
2								
3								
4								
5								
6								
7								
8								
9								
10					Love of Life			WHERE THE HEART IS
11								
12								
1/70								
2								
3								
4								
5								
6								
7								

	2:00p.m.	2:30p.m.	3:00p.m.	3:30p.m.	4:00p.m.	4:30p.m.	5:00p.m.	5:30p.m.
11	Love Is a	Art	To Tell	The Edge	Secret Storm			
12	Many	Linkletter's	the Truth	of Night	(cont.)			
1/68	Splendored	House Party	(cont.)	(cont.)				
	Thing	(cont.)						
	(cont.)							
2								
3								
4								
5								
6								
7								
8								
9								
10		Guiding	Secret Storm		Art			
11		Light			Linkletter's			
12					House Party			
1/69								
2								
3								
4								
5								
6								
7								
8								
9					GOMER PYLE			
10								
11								
12								
1/70								
2								
3								
4								
5								
6								
7								

110 / *Daytime CBS Schedule*

	10:00a.m.	10:30a.m.	11:00a.m.	11:30a.m.	12:00noon	12:30p.m.	1:00p.m.	1:30p.m.
8	The Lucy Show (cont.)	Beverly Hillbillies (cont.)	Andy Griffith Show (cont.)	Love of Life (cont.)		Search For Tomorrow (cont.)	Where the Heart Is (cont.)	As the World Turns (cont.)
9			FAMILY AFFAIR					
10								
11								
12		MY THREE SONS						
1/72								
2								
3								
4								
5								
6								
7		Beverly Hillbillies						
8								
9	JOKER IS WILD	THE PRICE IS RIGHT	GAMBIT					
10								
11								
12								
1/73								
2								
3								
4		$10,000 PYRAMID					Secret Storm	

	2:00p.m.	2:30p.m.	3:00p.m.	3:30p.m.	4:00p.m.	4:30p.m.	5:00p.m.	5:30p.m.
8	Love Is a	Guiding	Secret Storm	The Edge	Gomer Pyle			
	Many	Light	(cont.)	of Night	(cont.)			
9	Splendored	(cont.)		(cont.)				
	Thing							
10	(cont.)							
11								
12								
1/71								
2								
3								
4								
5								
6								
7								
8								
9								
10								
11								
12								
1/72								
2								
3					AMATEUR'S			
					GUIDE TO			
4					LOVE			
5								
6								
7					My Three			
					Sons			
8								
9	Guiding Light	The Edge	Love Is a	Secret Storm	Family			
		of Night	Many		Affair			
10			Splendored					
			Thing					
11								
12								
1/73					VIN SCULLY			
					SHOW			
2								
3								
4			The Price	HOLLYWOOD'S	THE YOUNG &			
			Is Right	TALKING	THE RESTLESS			

	10:00a.m.	10:30a.m.	11:00a.m.	11:30a.m.	12:00noon	12:30p.m.	1:00p.m.	1:30p.m.
5	Joker Is Wild (cont.)	$10,000 Pyramid (cont.)	Gambit (cont.)	Love of Life (cont.)		Search For Tomorrow (cont.)	Secret Storm (cont.)	As the World Turns (cont.)
6								
7								
8								
9							The Young & the	
10							Restless	
11								
12								
1/74								
2								
3								
4		Gambit	NOW YOU SEE IT					
5								
6								
7								
8								
9								
10								
11								
12								
1/75								
2								
3								
4								
5								
6	SPIN-OFF		Tattletales					
7								
8								
9	GIVE-N-TAKE	The Price Is Right	Gambit					
10								
11	Gambit	The Price Is Right						
12								As the World Turns
1/76								(to: 2:30)

	2:00p.m.	2:30p.m.	3:00p.m.	3:30p.m.	4:00p.m.	4:30p.m.	5:00p.m.	5:30p.m.
5	Guiding Light (cont.)	The Edge of Night (cont.)	The Price Is Right (cont.)	Hollywood's Talking (cont.)	The Young & The Restless (cont.)			
6								
7				MATCH GAME				
8								
9					Secret Storm			
10								
11								
12								
1/74								
2					TATTLETALES			
3								
4								
5								
6								
7								
8								
9								
10								
11								
12								
1/75								
2								
3								
4								
5								
6					MUSICAL CHAIRS			
7								
8								
9			Match Game	Tattletales				
10								
11					Give-n-Take			
12	As the World Turns (from: 1:30)	Guiding Light	ALL IN THE FAMILY	Match Game	Tattletales			
1/76								

	10:00a.m.	10:30a.m.	11:00a.m.	11:30a.m.	12:00noon	12:30p.m.	1:00p.m.	1:30p.m.
2	Gambit (cont.)	The Price Is Right (cont.)		Love of Life (cont.)		Search For Tomorrow	The Young & the Restless	As the World Turns
3						(cont.)	(cont.)	(to: 2:30) (cont.)
4								
5								
6								
7								
8								
9								
10								
11								
12	DOUBLE DARE							
1/77								
2								
3								
4					The Young & the Restless			
5	HERE'S LUCY							
6								
7								
8								
9								
10								
11	The Price Is Right		Match Game					
12	Tattletales	The Price Is Right						
1/78								
2								
3								
4	PASS THE BUCK							
5								
6								
7	TIC TAC DOUGH							
8								
9	All in the Family							
10								

	2:00p.m.	2:30p.m.	3:00p.m.	3:30p.m.	4:00p.m.	4:30p.m.	5:00p.m.	5:30p.m.
2	As the World	Guiding	All in the	Match Game	Tattletales			
	Turns	Light	Family	(cont.)	(cont.)			
3	(from: 1:30)	(cont.)	(cont.)					
	(cont.)							
4								
5								
6								
7								
8								
9								
10								
11								
12								
1/77								
2								
3								
4								
5								
6								
7								
8								
9								
10								
11		Guiding Light		All in the				
				Family				
12					Match Game			
1/78								
2								
3								
4								
5								
6								
7								
8								
9				M*A*S*H				
10								

	10:00a.m.	10:30a.m.	11:00a.m.	11:30a.m.	12:00noon	12:30p.m.	1:00p.m.	1:30p.m.
11	All in the	The Price Is Right (cont.)	Love of Life	The Young &	Search For			As the World
	Family		(cont.)	the	Tomorrow			Turns
12	(cont.)			Restless	(cont.)			(to: 2:30)
				(cont.)				(cont.)
1/79								
2								
3								
4		WHEW	The Price Is Right					
5								
6								
7								
8								
9	BEAT THE							
	CLOCK							
10								
11								
12								
1/80								
2	JEFFERSONS						The Young & the Restless	
3								
4								
5								
6		ALICE						
7								
8								
9								
10								
11								
12								
1/81								
2								
3								
4								
5								
6					The Young & the Restless			As the World
								Turns
7								(to: 2:30)

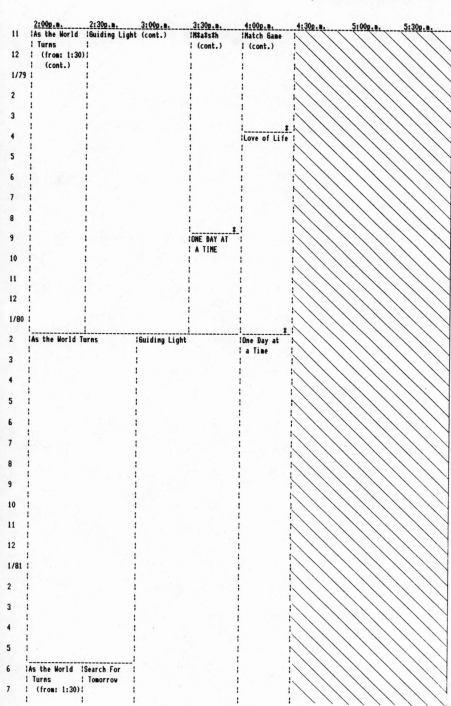

	2:00p.m.	2:30p.m.	3:00p.m.	3:30p.m.	4:00p.m.	4:30p.m.	5:00p.m.	5:30p.m.
11	As the World Turns	Guiding Light (cont.)		M*a*s*h (cont.)	Match Game (cont.)			
12	(from: 1:30) (cont.)							
1/79								
2								
3								
4					Love of Life			
5								
6								
7								
8								
9				ONE DAY AT A TIME				
10								
11								
12								
1/80								
2	As the World Turns		Guiding Light		One Day at a Time			
3								
4								
5								
6								
7								
8								
9								
10								
11								
12								
1/81								
2								
3								
4								
5								
6	As the World Turns	Search For Tomorrow						
7	(from: 1:30)							

	10:00a.m.	10:30a.m.	11:00a.m.	11:30a.m.	12:00noon	12:30p.m.	1:00p.m.	1:30p.m.
8	Jeffersons (cont.)	Alice (cont.)	The Price Is Right (cont.)		The Young & the Restless (cont.)			As the World Turns (to: 2:30) (cont.)
9								
10	One Day at a Time							
11								
12								
1/82								
2								
3								
4								
5								
6							The Young & the Restless	
7								
8								
9	$25,000 Pyramid	CHILD'S PLAY						
10								
11								
12								
1/83								
2								
3								
4								
5								
6								
7								
8								
9		PRESS YOUR LUCK						
10								
11								
12								
1/84								
2								
3								
4								

	2:00p.m.	2:30p.m.	3:00p.m.	3:30p.m.	4:00p.m.	4:30p.m.	5:00p.m.	5:30p.m.
8	As the World Turns	Search For Tomorrow	Guiding Light (cont.)		One Day at a Time			
9	(from: 1:30) (cont.)	(cont.)			(cont.)			
10					UP TO THE MINUTE			
11								
12					*			
1/82					Tattletales			
2								
3								
4		CAPITOL						
5								
6								
7								
8								
9								
10								
11								
12								
1/83								
2								
3								
4								
5								
6								
7					*			
8								
9								
10								
11								
12								
1/84								
2								
3								
4								

	10:00a.m.	10:30a.m.	11:00a.m.	11:30a.m.	12:00noon	12:30p.m.	1:00p.m.	1:30p.m.
5	$25,000 Pyramid (cont.)	Press Your Luck (cont.)	The Price Is Right (cont.)			The Young & the Restless (cont.)		As the World Turns (to:2:30) (cont.)
6								
7								
8								
9								
10								
11								
12								
1/85								
2								
3								
4								
5								
6								
7								
8								
9								
10								
11								
12								
1/86		NEW CARD SHARKS						
2								
3								
4								
5								
6								
7								
8								
9		CROSS WITS						
10								
11								
12								
1/87								

	2:00p.m.	2:30p.m.	3:00p.m.	3:30p.m.	4:00p.m.	4:30p.m.	5:00p.m.	5:30p.m.
5	As the World Turns	Capitol (cont.)	Guiding Light (cont.)					
6	(from: 1:30) (cont.)							
7								
8								
9								
10								
11								
12								
1/85								
2								
3								
4								
5								
6								
7								
8								
9								
10								
11								
12								
1/86								
2								
3								
4								
5								
6								
7								
8								
9								
10								
11								
12								
1/87								

	10:00a.m.	10:30a.m.	11:00a.m.	11:30a.m.	12:00noon	12:30p.m.	1:00p.m.	1:30p.m.
2	$25,000 Pyramid (cont.)	Cross Wits (cont.)	The Price Is Right (cont.)			The Young & the Restless (cont.)		AsWorldTurns (to:2:30-con)
3								THE BOLD
4								& THE
5								BEAUTIFUL
6		HOME SHOPPING GAME						
7								
8								
9								
10								
11								
12								
1/88	BLACKOUT	YAHTZEE						
2								
3								
4	$25,000 Pyramid	New Card Sharks						
5								
6								
7	FAMILY FEUD							
8								
9								
10								
11								
12								
1/89								
2								
3								
4		NOW YOU SEE IT						
5								
6								
7		Wheel of Fortune						
8								

	2:00p.m.	2:30p.m.	3:00p.m.	3:30p.m.	4:00p.m.	4:30p.m.	5:00p.m.	5:30p.m.
2	As World Turns	Capitol	Guiding Light (cont.)					
	(from1:30,con)	(cont.)	‡					
3	As the World Turns							
4								
5								
6								
7								
8								
9								
10								
11								
12								
1/88								
2								
3								
4								
5								
6								
7								
8								
9								
10								
11								
12								
1/89								
2								
3								
4								
5								
6								
7								
8								

Daytime CBS
Program Moves

Date	Time	Title (Minutes) – Type	Action	From/To
9/59	10:30	On the Go (30) – VY	x	
9/59	11:00	I Love Lucy (30) – SC	dp	
9/59	11:30	Top Dollar (30) – QU	x	
9/59	12:00	A Brighter Day (15) – SL	x	
9/59	12:15	Secret Storm (15) – SL	x	
9/59	12:30	Search for Tomorrow (15) – SL	x	
9/59	12:45	Guiding Light (15) – SL	x	
9/59	1:00	Love of Life (30) – SL	x	
9/59	1:30	As the World Turns (30) – SL	x	
9/59	2:00	For Better or Worse (30) – SL	x	
9/59	2:30	Art Linkletter's House Party(30) – TK	x	
9/59	3:00	Big Payoff (30) – QU	x	
9/59	3:30	The Verdict Is Yours (30) – CR	x	
9/59	4:30	Edge of Night (30) – SL	x	
10/59	11:30	Top Dollar (30) – QU	c	
10/59	3:00	Big Payoff (30) – QU	c	
11/59	11:30	December Bride (30) – SC	dp	
11/59	3:00	The Millionaire (30) – DR	dp	
11/59	4:00	Red Rowe Show (30) – VY	d	
6/60	2:00	For Better or Worse (30) – SL	c	
7/60	10:30	On the Go (30) – VY	c	
7/60	11:30	December Bride (30) – SC	cp	
7/60	2:00	Full Circle (30) – SL	d	
7/60	4:00	Red Rowe Show (30) – VY	c	
8/60	10:30	Video Village (30) – QU	d	
8/60	11:30	Clear Horizon (30) – SL	d	
3/61	11:00	I Love Lucy (30) – SC	m	To:10
3/61	11:30	Clear Horizon (30) – SL	m	To:11:30-3/62
3/61	2:00	Full Circle (30) – SL	c	
4/61	10:00	I Love Lucy (30) – SC	m	Fr:11
4/61	11:00	Double Exposure (30) – QU	d	
4/61	11:30	Your Surprise Package (30) – QU	d	
4/61	2:00	Face the Facts (30) – QU	d	
9/61	10:00	I Love Lucy (30) – SC	m	To:11

125

Date	Time	Title (Minutes) — Type	Action	From/To
9/61	11:00	Double Exposure (30) — QU	c	
9/61	2:00	Face the Facts (30) — QU	c	
10/61	10:00	Calendar (30) — MG	d	
10/61	11:00	I Love Lucy (30) — SC	m	Fr:10
10/61	2:00	Password (30) — QU	d	
2/62	11:30	Your Surprise Package (30) — QU	c	
3/62	11:30	Clear Horizon (30) — SL	m	Fr:11:30-3/61
6/62	10:30	Video Village (30) — QU	c	
6/62	11:00	I Love Lucy (30) — SC	m	To:10:30
6/62	11:30	Clear Horizon (30) — SL	c	
6/62	12:00	A Brighter Day (15) — SL	c	
6/62	12:15	Secret Storm (15) — SL	m	To:4
6/62	3:30	The Verdict Is Yours (30) — CR	m	To:11
6/62	4:30	Edge of Night (30) — SL	m	To:11:30
7/62	10:30	I Love Lucy (30) — SC	m	Fr:11
7/62	11:00	The Verdict Is Yours (30) — CR	m	Fr:3:30
7/62	11:30	Edge of Night (30) — SL	m	Fr:4:30
7/62	3:30	To Tell the Truth (30) — QU	d	
7/62	4:00	Secret Storm (30) — SL	m	Fr:12:15
9/62	11:00	The Verdict Is Yours (30) — CR	c	
10/62	11:00	The Real McCoys (30) — SC	dp	
11/62	11:30	Edge of Night (30) — SL	m	To:4:30
12/62	11:30	Love That Bob (30) — SC	m	Fr:11:30-11/61(a)
12/62	3:00	The Millionaire (30) — DR	m	To:3:30
12/62	3:30	To Tell the Truth (30) — QU	m	To:3
12/62	4:30	Edge of Night (30) — SL	m	Fr:11:30
1/63	3:00	To Tell the Truth (30) — QU	m	Fr:3:30
1/63	3:30	The Millionaire (30) — DR	m	Fr:3
6/63	3:30	The Millionaire (30) — DR	m	To:4:30
6/63	4:30	Edge of Night (30) — SL	m	To:3:30
7/63	3:30	Edge of Night (30) — SL	m	Fr:4:30
7/63	4:30	The Millionaire (30) — DR	m	Fr:3:30
8/63	10:00	Calendar (30) — MG	c	
8/63	4:30	The Millionaire (30) — DR	cp	
9/64	11:00	The Real McCoys (30) — SC	m	To:10
10/64	10:00	The Real McCoys (30) — SC	m	Fr:11
10/64	11:00	Andy Griffith Show (30) — SC	dp	
7/65	10:30	I Love Lucy (30) — SC	m	To:10:30-1/66
7/65	11:30	Love That Bob (30) — SC	m	To:10:30
8/65	10:30	Love That Bob (30) — SC	m	Fr:11:30
8/65	10:30	Love That Bob (30) — SC	cp	
8/65	11:30	Dick Van Dyke Show (30) — SC	dp	
9/65	10:30	P.D.Q. (30) — QU	d	
12/65	10:30	P.D.Q. (30) — QU	c	
1/66	10:30	I Love Lucy (30) — SC	m	Fr:10:30-7/65
9/66	10:00	The Real McCoys (30) — SC	cp	
9/66	10:30	I Love Lucy (30) — SC	m	To:10
10/66	10:00	I Love Lucy (30) — SC	m	Fr:10:30
10/66	10:30	Beverly Hillbillies (30) — SC	dp	
9/67	10:00	I Love Lucy (30) — SC	cp	

Date	Time	Title (Minutes)—Type	Action	From/To
9/67	2:00	Password (30)—QU	m	To:4-4/71(a)
10/67	10:00	Petticoat Junction (30)—SC	dp	
10/67	2:00	Love Is a Many Splendored Thing (30)—SL	d	
8/68	10:00	Petticoat Junction (30)—SC	cp	
9/68	10:00	Lucy Show (30)—SC	dp	
9/68	12:30	Search for Tomorrow (15)—SL	m	To:12:30(30min)
9/68	12:45	Guiding Light (15)—SL	m	To:2:30
9/68	2:30	Art Linkletter's House Party (30)—TK	m	To:4
9/68	3:00	To Tell the Truth (30)—QU	c	
9/68	4:00	Secret Storm (30)—SL	m	To:3
10/68	12:30	Search for Tomorrow (30)—SL	m	Fr:12:30(15min)
10/68	2:30	Guiding Light (30)—SL	m	Fr:12:45
10/68	3:00	Secret Storm (30)—SL	m	Fr:4
10/68	4:00	Art Linkletter's House Party (30)—TK	m	Fr:2:30
8/69	4:00	Art Linkletter's House Party (30)—TK	c	
9/69	11:30	Dick Van Dyke Show (30)—SC	cp	
9/69	1:00	Love of Life (30)—SL	m	To:11:30
9/69	4:00	Gomer Pyle (30)—SC	dp	
10/69	11:30	Love of Life (30)—SL	m	Fr:1
10/69	1:00	Where the Heart Is (30)—SL	d	
9/70	11:00	Andy Griffith Show (30)—SC	cp	
10/70	11:00	Family Affair (30)—SC	dp	
11/71	10:30	Beverly Hillbillies (30)—SC	m	To:10:30-7/72
12/71	10:30	My Three Sons (30)—SC	dp	
2/72	4:00	Gomer Pyle (30)—SC	cp	
3/72	4:00	Amateur's Guide to Love (30)—QU	d	
6/72	10:30	My Three Sons (30)—SC	m	To:4
6/72	4:00	Amateur's Guide to Love (30)—QU	c	
7/72	10:30	Beverly Hillbillies (30)—SC	m	Fr:10:30-11/71
7/72	4:00	My Three Sons (30)—SC	m	Fr:10:30
8/72	10:00	Lucy Show (30)—SC	cp	
8/72	10:30	Beverly Hillbillies (30)—SC	cp	
8/72	11:00	Family Affair (30)—SC	m	To:4
8/72	2:00	Love Is a Many Splendored Thing —(30)—SL	m	To:3
8/72	2:30	Guiding Light (30)—SL	m	To:2
8/72	3:00	Secret Storm (30)—SL	m	To:3:30
8/72	3:30	Edge of Night (30)—SL	m	To:2:30
8/72	4:00	My Three Sons (30)—SC	cp	
9/72	10:00	Joker Is Wild (30)—QU	d	
9/72	10:30	The Price Is Right (30)—QU	d	
9/72	11:00	Gambit (30)—QU	d	
9/72	2:00	Guiding Light (30)—SL	m	Fr:2:30
9/72	2:30	Edge of Night (30)—SL	m	Fr:3:30
9/72	3:00	Love Is a Many Splendored Thing (30)—SL	m	Fr:2

Date	Time	Title (Minutes) — Type	Action	From/To
9/72	3:30	Secret Storm (30) — SL	m	Fr:3
9/72	4:00	Family Affair (30) — SC	m	Fr:11
12/72	4:00	Family Affair (30) — SC	cp	
1/73	4:00	Vin Scully Show (30) — VY	d	
3/73	10:30	The Price Is Right (30) — QU	m	To:3
3/73	1:00	Where the Heart Is (30) — SL	c	
3/73	3:00	Love Is a Many Splendored Thing (30) — SL	c	
3/73	3:30	Secret Storm (30) — SL	m	To:1
3/73	4:00	Vin Scully Show (30) — VY	c	
4/73	10:30	$10,000 Pyramid (30) — QU	d	
4/73	1:00	Secret Storm (30) — SL	m	Fr:3:30
4/73	3:00	The Price Is Right (30) — QU	m	Fr:10:30
4/73	3:30	Hollywood's Talking (30) — QU	d	
4/73	4:00	The Young & the Restless (30) — SL	d	
6/73	3:30	Hollywood's Talking (30) — QU	c	
7/73	3:30	Match Game (30) — QU	d	
8/73	1:00	Secret Storm (30) — SL	m	To:4
8/73	4:00	The Young & the Restless (30) — SL	m	To:1
9/73	1:00	The Young & the Restless (30) — SL	m	Fr:4
9/73	4:00	Secret Storm (30) — SL	m	Fr:1
1/74	4:00	Secret Storm (30) — SL	c	
2/74	4:00	Tattletales (30) — QU	d	
3/74	10:30	$10,000 Pyramid (30) — QU	m	To:11-5/74(a)
3/74	11:00	Gambit (30) — QU	m	To:10:30
4/74	10:30	Gambit (30) — QU	m	Fr:11
4/74	11:00	Now You See It (30) — QU	d	
5/75	10:00	Joker Is Wild (30) — QU	c	
5/75	11:00	Now You See It (30) — QU	c	
5/75	4:00	Tattletales (30) — QU	m	To:11
6/75	10:00	Spin-Off (30) — QU	d	
6/75	11:00	Tattletales (30) — QU	m	Fr:4
6/75	4:00	Musical Chairs (30) — QU	d	
8/75	10:00	Spin-Off (30) — QU	c	
8/75	10:30	Gambit (30) — QU	m	To:11
8/75	11:00	Tattletales (30) — QU	m	To:3:30
8/75	3:00	The Price Is Right (30) — QU	m	To:10:30
8/75	3:30	Match Game (30) — QU	m	To:3
9/75	10:00	Give-N-Take (30) — QU	d	
9/75	10:30	The Price Is Right (30) — QU	m	Fr:3
9/75	11:00	Gambit (30) — QU	m	Fr:10:30
9/75	3:00	Match Game (30) — QU	m	Fr:3:30
9/75	3:30	Tattletales (30) — QU	m	Fr:11
10/75	10:00	Give-N-Take (30) — QU	m	To:4
10/75	10:30	The Price Is Right (30) — QU	m	To:10:30(60min)
10/75	11:00	Gambit (30) — QU	m	To:10
10/75	4:00	Musical Chairs (30) — QU	c	
11/75	10:00	Gambit (30) — QU	m	Fr:11
11/75	10:30	The Price Is Right (60) — QU	m	Fr:10:30(30min)
11/75	1:30	As the World Turns (30) — SL	m	To:1:30(60min)

Date	Time	Title (Minutes) — Type	Action	From/To
11/75	2:00	Guiding Light (30) — SL	m	To:2:30
11/75	2:30	Edge of Night (30) — SL	m	To:4(abc)
11/75	3:00	Match Game (30) — QU	m	To:3:30
11/75	3:30	Tattletales (30) — QU	m	To:4
11/75	4:00	Give-N-Take (30) — QU	m	Fr:10
11/75	4:00	Give-N-Take (30) — QU	c	
12/75	1:30	As the World Turns (60) — SL	m	Fr:1:30(30min)
12/75	2:30	Guiding Light (30) — SL	m	Fr:2
12/75	3:00	All in the Family (30) — SC	dp	
12/75	3:30	Match Game (30) — QU	m	Fr:3
12/75	4:00	Tattletales (30) — QU	m	Fr:3:30
11/76	10:00	Gambit (30) — QU	c	
12/76	10:00	Double Dare (30) — QU	d	
3/77	1:00	The Young & the Restless (30) — SL	m	To:12
4/77	10:00	Double Dare (30) — QU	c	
4/77	12:00	The Young & the Restless (30) — SL	m	Fr:1
5/77	10:00	Here's Lucy (30) — SC	dp	
10/77	10:00	Here's Lucy (30) — SC	cp	
10/77	10:30	The Price Is Right (60) — QU	m	To:10
10/77	2:30	Guiding Light (30) — SL	m	To:2:30(60min)
10/77	3:00	All in the Family (30) — SC	m	To:3:30
10/77	3:30	Match Game (30) — QU	m	To:11
11/77	10:00	The Price Is Right (60) — QU	m	Fr:10:30
11/77	10:00	The Price Is Right (60) — QU	m	To:10:30
11/77	11:00	Match Game (30) — QU	m	Fr:3:30
11/77	11:00	Match Game (30) — QU	m	To:4
11/77	2:30	Guiding Light (60) — SL	m	Fr:2:30(30min)
11/77	3:30	All in the Family (30) — SC	m	Fr:3
11/77	4:00	Tattletales (30) — QU	m	To:10
12/77	10:00	Tattletales (30) — QU	m	Fr:4
12/77	10:30	The Price Is Right (60) — QU	m	Fr:10
12/77	4:00	Match Game (30) — QU	m	Fr:11
3/78	10:00	Tattletales (30) — QU	m	To:4-1/82
4/78	10:00	Pass the Buck (30) — QU	d	
6/78	10:00	Pass the Buck (30) — QU	c	
7/78	10:00	Tic Tac Dough (30) — QU	d	
8/78	10:00	Tic Tac Dough (30) — QU	c	
8/78	3:30	All in the Family (30) — SC	m	To:10
9/78	10:00	All in the Family (30) — SC	m	Fr:3:30
9/78	3:30	M*A*S*H (30) — SC	dp	
3/79	10:30	The Price Is Right (60) — QU	m	To:11
3/79	11:30	Love of Life (30) — SL	m	To:4
3/79	4:00	Match Game (30) — QU	c	
4/79	10:30	Whew (30) — QU	d	
4/79	11:00	The Price Is Right (60) — QU	m#	Fr:10:30
4/79	4:00	Love of Life (30) — SL	m	Fr:11:30
8/79	10:00	All in the Family (30) — SC	cp	
8/79	3:30	M*A*S*H (30) — SC	cp	
9/79	10:00	Beat the Clock (30) — QU	d	
9/79	3:30	One Day at a Time (30) — SC	dp	

Date	Time	Title (Minutes)—Type	Action	From/To
1/80	10:00	Beat the Clock (30)—QU	c	
1/80	12:00	The Young & the Restless (30)—SL	m	To:1
1/80	1:30	As the World Turns (60)—SL	m	To:2
1/80	2:30	Guiding Light (60)—SL	m	To:3
1/80	3:30	One Day at a Time (30)—SC	m	To:4
1/80	4:00	Love of Life (30)—SL	c	
2/80	10:00	The Jeffersons (30)—SC	dp	
2/80	1:00	The Young & the Restless (60)—SL	m	Fr:12
2/80	2:00	As the World Turns (60)—SL	m	Fr:1:30
2/80	3:00	Guiding Light (60)—SL	m#	Fr:2:30
2/80	4:00	One Day at a Time (30)—SC	m	Fr:3:30
5/80	10:30	Whew (30)—QU	c	
6/80	10:30	Alice (30)—SC	dp	
5/81	12:30	Search for Tomorrow (30)—SL	m	To:2:30
5/81	1:00	The Young & the Restless (60)—SL	m	To:12
5/81	2:00	As the World Turns (60)—SL	m	To:1:30
6/81	12:00	The Young & the Restless (60)—SL	m	Fr:1
6/81	1:30	As the World Turns (60)—SL	m	Fr:2
6/81	2:30	Search for Tomorrow (30)—SL	m	Fr:12:30
9/81	10:00	The Jeffersons (30)—SC	cp	
9/81	4:00	One Day at a Time (30)—SC	m	To:10
10/81	10:00	One Day at a Time (30)—SC	m	Fr:4
10/81	4:00	Up to the Minute (30)—NM	d	
12/81	4:00	Up to the Minute (30)—NM	c	
1/82	4:00	Tattletales (30)—QU	m	Fr:10-3/78
3/82	2:30	Search for Tomorrow (30)—SL	m	To:12:30(n)
4/82	2:30	Capitol (30)—SL	d	
5/82	12:00	The Young & the Restless (60)—SL	m	To:12:30
6/82	12:30	The Young & the Restless (60)—SL	m#	Fr:12
8/82	10:00	One Day at a Time (30)—SC	cp	
8/82	10:30	Alice (30)—SC	cp	
9/82	10:00	$25,000 Pyramid (30)—QU	m	Fr:12-6/80(a)
9/82	10:30	Child's Play (30)—QU	d	
7/83	4:00	Tattletales (30)—QU	c	
8/83	10:30	Child's Play (30)—QU	c	
9/83	10:30	Press Your Luck (30)—QU	d	
12/85	10:30	Press Your Luck (30)—QU	c	
1/86	10:30	New Card Sharks (30)—QU	d	
8/86	10:30	New Card Sharks (30)—QU	m	To:10:30-4/88
9/86	10:30	Cross Wits (30)—QU	d	
2/87	1:30	As the World Turns (60)—SL	m	To:2
2/87	2:30	Capitol (30)—SL	c	
3/87	1:30	Bold and the Beautiful (30)—SL	d#	
3/87	2:00	As the World Turns (60)—SL	m#	Fr:1:30
5/87	10:30	Cross Wits (30)—QU	c	
6/87	10:30	Home Shopping Game (30)—QU	d	
12/87	10:00	$25,000 Pyramid (30)—QU	m	To:10-4/88
12/87	10:30	Home Shopping Game (30)—QU	c	
1/88	10:00	Blackout (30)—QU	d	
1/88	10:30	Yahtzee (30)—QU	d	

Date	Time	Title (Minutes) — Type	Action	From/To
3/88	10:00	Blackout (30) — QU	c	
3/88	10:30	Yahtzee (30) — QU	c	
4/88	10:00	$25,000 Pyramid (30) — QU	m	Fr:10-12/87
4/88	10:30	New Card Sharks (30) — QU	m	Fr:10:30-8/86
6/88	10:00	$25,000 Pyramid (30) — QU	c	
7/88	10:00	Family Feud (30) — QU	d#	
3/89	10:30	New Card Sharks (30) — QU	c	
4/89	10:30	Now You See It (30) — QU	d	
6/89	10:30	Now You See It (30) — QU	c	
7/89	10:30	Wheel of Fortune (30) — QU	m#	Fr:11(n)

Daytime CBS
Programming Moves Summary

1959–60

Series Premieres: December Bride; Full Circle; I Love Lucy; The Millionaire; The Red Rowe Show. *Key Programming Moves:* CBS began airing reruns of two of its most successful prime-time series, I LOVE LUCY in the 11–11:30 a.m. slot, and DECEMBER BRIDE in the 11:30–12 noon slot. I LOVE LUCY would continue to run on CBS' daytime schedule until September 1967, while DECEMBER BRIDE was removed from the schedule at the end of the season. Reruns of another successful CBS prime-time series, THE MILLIONAIRE, debuted in November; it remained part of CBS' daytime schedule for the next four years. A new soap opera, FULL CIRCLE, replaced FOR BETTER OR WORSE in the 2–2:30 slot in July; it lasted only eight months. TOP DOLLAR and THE BIG PAYOFF were cancelled in October. ON THE GO and THE RED ROWE SHOW were cancelled in July.

1960–61

Series Premieres: Clear Horizon; Double Exposure; Face the Facts; Video Village; Your Surprise Package. *Key Programming Moves:* In April, CBS expanded its daytime schedule by moving I LOVE LUCY into the 10–10:30 a.m. slot. Also in April, CBS cancelled the short-lived soap opera FULL CIRCLE, which occupied the 2–2:30 p.m. slot, and scheduled a quiz program (FACE THE FACTS) in this slot for the first time. FACE THE FACTS, too, was short-lived, being cancelled at the end of the season.

1961–62

Series Premieres: Calendar; Password; To Tell the Truth. *Key Programming Moves:* CALENDAR debuted in the 10–10:30 a.m. slot; this magazine program was moderately successful, lasting for two years. PASSWORD debuted; this highly successful quiz program remained part of CBS' daytime schedule until the end of the 1966–67 season. TO TELL THE TRUTH debuted in July; this series remained part of the CBS daytime lineup until the end of the 1967–68 season. In July, SECRET STORM was expanded from 15 minutes to 30 minutes and moved into the 4–4:30 p.m. slot, which it would occupy until September 1968. Also in July, A BRIGHTER DAY was cancelled, and CBS ceased programming the 12–12:30 p.m. slot.

1962–63

Series Premieres: The Real McCoys. *Key Programming Moves:* THE REAL McCOYS moved from ABC's prime-time schedule to CBS' prime-time schedule at the beginning of the 1962–63 season. As a consequence, CBS began airing reruns of the episodes that originally aired on ABC as part of its daytime schedule, in addition to airing new episodes in prime-time. In January, TO TELL THE TRUTH was moved into the 3–3:30 p.m. slot, and in July THE EDGE OF NIGHT was moved into the 3:30–4 p.m. slot, thus stabilizing the CBS daytime schedule for the next several years. THE MILLIONAIRE and CALENDAR were cancelled at the end of the season.

1963–64

Key Programming Moves: CBS ceased to air programming in the 10–10:30 a.m. and the 4:30–5 p.m. slots during this season.

1964–65

Series Premieres: The Andy Griffith Show. *Key Programming Moves:* THE REAL McCOYS was moved to 10:00 a.m. as CBS resumed programming in the 10–10:30 a.m. slot. Reruns of prime-time's THE ANDY GRIFFITH SHOW debuted in the 11–11:30 a.m. slot, where they would run until September 1970.

1965–66

Series Premieres: The Dick Van Dyke Show; P.D.Q. *Key Programming Moves:* Continuing its successful practice of airing reruns of its top prime-time situation comedies as part of its morning schedule, CBS began airing THE DICK VAN DYKE SHOW reruns in the 11:30–12 noon slot. CBS cancelled THE REAL McCOYS at the end of the season.

1966–67

Series Premieres: The Beverly Hillbillies. *Key Programming Moves:* CBS began airing reruns of prime-time's THE BEVERLY HILLBILLIES in the 10:30–11 a.m. slot, which would occupy this slot for the next six years. Two long-running series left CBS' schedule at the end of the season; PASSWORD and I LOVE LUCY were cancelled. PASSWORD would return on ABC in several years.

1967–68

Series Premieres: Love Is a Many Splendored Thing; Petticoat Junction. *Key Programming Moves:* CBS offered a new soap opera, LOVE IS A MANY SPLENDORED THING; it became a modest success and stayed on the schedule until March 1973. After a successful six-year run, TO TELL THE TRUTH was cancelled at the end of the season.

1968–69

Series Premieres: The Lucy Show. *Key Programming Moves:* Lucille Ball returned to CBS' daytime lineup as reruns of prime-time's THE LUCY SHOW aired in the 10–10:30 a.m. slot; it occupied this slot for the next four years. Two of CBS' longest-running soap operas, SEARCH FOR TOMORROW and THE GUIDING LIGHT were expanded to 30 minutes. SEARCH FOR TOMORROW continued to air at 12:30 p.m., while THE GUIDING LIGHT moved to 2:30 p.m., replacing ART LINKLETTER'S HOUSE PARTY which was moved to 4:00 p.m. CBS now had a 3½-hour block of soap operas (12:30–4 p.m.). ART LINKLETTER'S HOUSE PARTY and DICK VAN DYKE SHOW were cancelled at the end of the season.

1969–70

Series Premieres: Gomer Pyle, USMC; Where the Heart Is. *Key Programming Moves:* LOVE OF LIFE was moved from the 1–1:30 p.m. slot, which it occupied for over 15 years, to the 11:30–12 noon slot; it stayed in the new slot for almost 10 years. THE ANDY GRIFFITH SHOW was cancelled at the end of the season.

1970–71

Series Premieres: Family Affair. *Key Programming Moves:* CBS' daytime schedule remained intact for the 1970–71 season.

1971–72

Series Premieres: The Amateur's Guide to Love; My Three Sons. *Key Programming Moves:* THE LUCY SHOW and THE BEVERLY HILLBILLIES were cancelled at the end of the season.

1972–73

Series Premieres: Gambit; Hollywood's Talking; The Joker Is Wild; The Match Game; The Price Is Right; The $10,000 Pyramid; The Vin Scully Show; The Young and the Restless. *Key Programming Moves:* CBS shook up its daytime lineup, offering many new series, and switching time slots of returning shows. CBS offered many new quiz programs. Three of the new quiz shows caught on — THE JOKER IS WILD, GAMBIT and THE $10,000 PYRAMID. In addition, CBS offered new versions of two previously successful quiz shows — THE PRICE IS RIGHT and THE MATCH GAME returned to daytime schedules and immediately caught on with the audience. CBS also offered up a new soap opera, THE YOUNG AND THE RESTLESS, designed to appeal to a younger audience; it caught on and became a mainstay on the CBS schedule. LOVE IS A MANY SPLENDORED THING was cancelled in March.

1973–74

Series Premieres: Now You See It; Tattletales. *Key Programming Moves:* THE YOUNG AND THE RESTLESS and THE SECRET STORM switched time slots — STORM moving from 1–1:30 p.m. to 4–4:30 p.m. In January,

SECRET STORM was cancelled. TATTLETALES debuted in February. The $10,000 PYRAMID was dropped by CBS in March; it was subsequently picked up by ABC.

1974–75

Series Premieres: Musical Chairs; Spin-Off. *Key Programming Moves:* THE JOKER IS WILD was cancelled in May.

1975–76

Series Premieres: All in the Family; Give-N-Take. *Key Programming Moves:* In November, THE PRICE IS RIGHT expanded to 60 minutes. Reruns of prime-time's ALL IN THE FAMILY debuted in December. Also in December, AS THE WORLD TURNS expanded to 60 minutes.

1976–77

Series Premieres: Double Dare; Here's Lucy. *Key Programming Moves:* GAMBIT was cancelled in November.

1977–78

Series Premieres: Pass the Buck; Tic Tac Dough. *Key Programming Moves:* In November, THE GUIDING LIGHT was expanded to one hour.

1978–79

Series Premieres: M*A*S*H; Whew. *Key Programming Moves:* Reruns of prime-time's M*A*S*H debuted; it was cancelled at the end of the season. ALL IN THE FAMILY was moved into the 10–10:30 a.m. lead-off slot at the beginning of the season; it was cancelled at season's end. THE MATCH GAME was cancelled in March. In April, LOVE OF LIFE was moved from its 11:30 a.m. slot into the 4:00 p.m. slot.

1979–80

Series Premieres: Alice; Beat the Clock; The Jeffersons; One Day at a Time. *Key Programming Moves:* In an attempt to bolster a sagging lineup, CBS imported reruns of three of its most successful prime-time series — THE JEFFERSONS, ONE DAY AT A TIME and ALICE; they didn't provide much help. After 30 years, LOVE OF LIFE was cancelled in January.

1980–81

Key Programming Moves: THE JEFFERSONS was cancelled at the end of the season.

1981–82

Series Premieres: Capitol; Up to the Minute. *Key Programming Moves:* CAPITOL debuted in April; this soap opera became a modest hit, lasting nearly five years. In March, SEARCH FOR TOMORROW, after 31 years on CBS, was picked up by NBC. ALICE and ONE DAY AT A TIME were cancelled at the end of the season.

1982–83

Series Premieres: Child's Play. *Key Programming Moves:* CBS brought THE $25,000 PYRAMID back to network daytime television; it remained on CBS' schedule for the next five years. TATTLETALES was cancelled in July; CBS did not resume programming in the 4–4:30 p.m. slot.

1983–84

Series Premieres: Press Your Luck. *Key Programming Moves:* CBS' daytime schedule remained relatively intact during the 1983–84 season.

1984–85

Key Programming Moves: CBS' daytime schedule remained relatively intact during the 1984–85 season.

1985–86

Series Premieres: The New Card Sharks. *Key Programming Moves:* PRESS YOUR LUCK was cancelled in December; otherwise CBS' daytime schedule remained relatively intact during the 1985–86 season.

1986–87

Series Premieres: The Bold and the Beautiful; Cross Wits; The Home Shopping Game. *Key Programming Moves:* CAPITOL was cancelled in February. CBS' newest soap opera, THE BOLD AND THE BEAUTIFUL debuted in March; it performed moderately well.

1987–88

Series Premieres: Blackout; Family Feud; Yahtzee. *Key Programming Moves:* A new version of the once successful FAMILY FEUD was introduced in July; while not performing up to the level of its predecessor, it still performed admirably for CBS.

1988–89

Series Premieres: Now You See It. *Key Programming Moves:* In July, CBS wooed the highly successful WHEEL OF FORTUNE away from NBC and made it part of its daytime schedule.

NBC Daytime

September 1959–August 1989

	10:00a.m.	10:30a.m.	11:00a.m.	11:30a.m.	12:00noon	12:30p.m.	1:00p.m.	1:30p.m.
9/59	Dough Re Mi	Treasure Hunt	The Price Is Right	Concentration	Tic Tac Dough	It Could Be You	SPLIT PERSONALITY	Queen For a Day
10								
11								
12					Truth Or Consequences			
1/60		PLAY YOUR HUNCH						
2								
3								
4								
5								
6								
7								
8								
9								
10							CHARGE ACCOUNT	HERE'S HOLLYWOOD
11								
12								
1/61	SAY WHEN							
2								
3								
4								
5								
6								
7								
8								
9								
10								
11								
12								
1/62					YOUR FIRST IMPRESSION	Truth Or Consequences		
2								
3								
4								

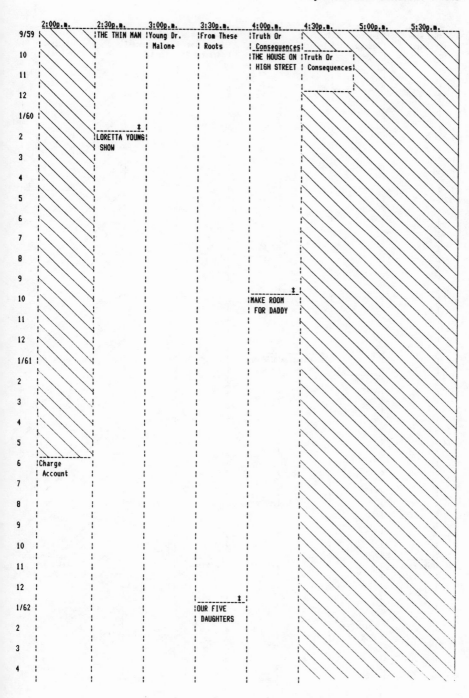

	2:00p.m.	2:30p.m.	3:00p.m.	3:30p.m.	4:00p.m.	4:30p.m.	5:00p.m.	5:30p.m.
9/59		THE THIN MAN	Young Dr. Malone	From These Roots	Truth Or Consequences			
10					THE HOUSE ON HIGH STREET	Truth Or Consequences		
11								
12								
1/60								
2		LORETTA YOUNG SHOW						
3								
4								
5								
6								
7								
8								
9								
10					MAKE ROOM FOR DADDY			
11								
12								
1/61								
2								
3								
4								
5								
6	Charge Account							
7								
8								
9								
10								
11								
12								
1/62				OUR FIVE DAUGHTERS				
2								
3								
4								

	10:00a.m.	10:30a.m.	11:00a.m.	11:30a.m.	12:00noon	12:30p.m.	1:00p.m.	1:30p.m.
5	Say When (cont.)	Play Your Hunch (cont.)	The Price Is Right (cont.)	Concentration (cont.)	Your First Impression (cont.)	Truth Or Consequences (cont.)		Here's Hollywood (cont.)
6								
7								
8								
9								
10								
11								
12								
1/63								
2								
3								
4								
5								
6								
7								
8								
9			Concentration	MISSING LINKS				
10		WORD FOR WORD						
11								
12								
1/64								
2								
3								
4				JEOPARDY				
5								
6								
7	Make Room For Daddy				Say When			Let's Make a Deal
8								
9								
10		WHAT'S THIS SONG						
11								
12								
1/65								

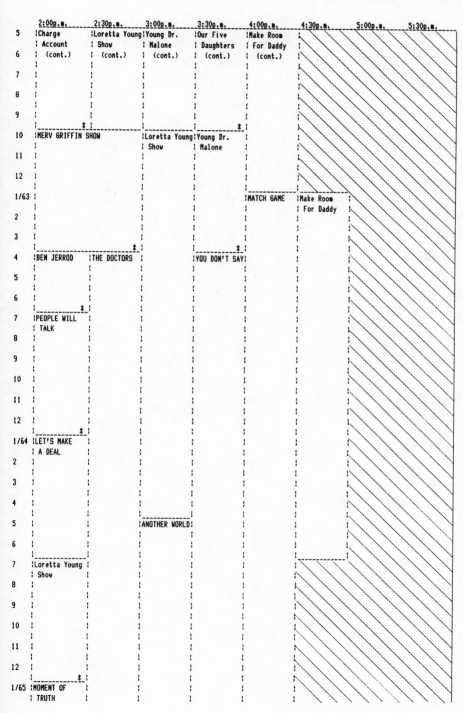

	2:00p.m.	2:30p.m.	3:00p.m.	3:30p.m.	4:00p.m.	4:30p.m.	5:00p.m.	5:30p.m.
5	Charge Account (cont.)	Loretta Young Show (cont.)	Young Dr. Malone (cont.)	Our Five Daughters (cont.)	Make Room For Daddy (cont.)			
6								
7								
8								
9								
10	MERV GRIFFIN SHOW		Loretta Young Show	Young Dr. Malone				
11								
12								
1/63					MATCH GAME	Make Room For Daddy		
2								
3								
4	BEN JERROD	THE DOCTORS		YOU DON'T SAY				
5								
6								
7	PEOPLE WILL TALK							
8								
9								
10								
11								
12								
1/64	LET'S MAKE A DEAL							
2								
3								
4								
5			ANOTHER WORLD					
6								
7	Loretta Young Show							
8								
9								
10								
11								
12								
1/65	MOMENT OF TRUTH							

	10:00a.m.	10:30a.m.	11:00a.m.	11:30a.m.	12:00noon	12:30p.m.	1:00p.m.	1:30p.m.
2	Make Room For Daddy	What's This Song	Concentration (cont.)	Jeopardy (cont.)	Say When (cont.)	Truth Or Consequences		Let's Make a Deal
3	(cont.)	(cont.)				(cont.)		(cont.)
4	Truth Or Consequences				CALL MY BLUFF	I'LL BET		
5								
6								
7								
8								
9	FRACTURED PHRASES	Concentration	MORNING STAR	PARADISE BAY	Jeopardy	LET'S PLAY POST OFFICE		
10								
11								
12								
1/66	EYE GUESS							
2								
3								
4								
5								
6								
7								
8			CHAIN LETTER	SHOWDOWN		SWINGIN' COUNTRY		
9								
10								
11			PAT BOONE SHOW	HOLLYWOOD SQUARES				
12								
1/67	REACH FOR THE STARS					Eye Guess		
2								
3								
4	SNAP JUDGMENT							
5								
6								
7			PERSONALITY					
8								
9								
10								

	2:00p.m.	2:30p.m.	3:00p.m.	3:30p.m.	4:00p.m.	4:30p.m.	5:00p.m.	5:30p.m.
2	Moment of	The Doctors	Another	You Don't Say	Match Game			
	Truth	(cont.)	World	(cont.)	(cont.)			
3	(cont.)		(cont.)					
4								
5								
6								
7								
8								
9								
10								
11	DAYS OF OUR							
	LIVES							
12								
1/66								
2								
3								
4								
5								
6								
7								
8								
9								
10								
11								
12								
1/67								
2								
3								
4								
5								
6								
7								
8								
9								
10								

	10:00a.m.	10:30a.m.	11:00a.m.	11:30a.m.	12:00noon	12:30p.m.	1:00p.m.	1:30p.m.
11	Snap	Concentration	Personality	Hollywood	Jeopardy	Eye Guess		Let's Make
	Judgment	(cont.)	(cont.)	Squares	(cont.)	(cont.)		a Deal
12	(cont.)			(cont.)				(cont.)
1/68								
2								
3								
4								
5								
6								
7								
8								
9								
10								
11								
12								
1/69								HIDDEN FACES
2								
3								
4	IT TAKES TWO							
5								
6								
7								YOU'RE
8								PUTTING
								ME ON
9								
10			SALE OF THE			NAME DROPPERS		
			CENTURY					
11								
12								
1/70						WHO, WHAT		LIFE WITH
						OR WHERE		LINKLETTER
2								
3								
4								
5								
6								
7								

	2:00p.m.	2:30p.m.	3:00p.m.	3:30p.m.	4:00p.m.	4:30p.m.	5:00p.m.	5:30p.m.
11	Days of Our	The Doctors	Another	You Don't Say	Match Game			
	Lives	(cont.)	World	(cont.)	(cont.)			
12	(cont.)		(cont.)					
1/68								
2								
3								
4								
5								
6								
7								
8								
9								
10								
11								
12								
1/69								
2								
3								
4								
5								
6								
7								
8								
9								
10				BRIGHT	LETTERS TO			
				PROMISE	LAUGH-IN			
11								
12								
1/70					Name			
2					Droppers			
3								
4					SOMERSET			
5								
6								
7								

	10:00a.m.	10:30a.m.	11:00a.m.	11:30a.m.	12:00noon	12:30p.m.	1:00p.m.	1:30p.m.
8	DINAH'S PLACE	Concentration	Sale of the	Hollywood	Jeopardy	Who, What		Life With
		(cont.)	Century	Squares	(cont.)	Or Where		Linkletter
9			(cont.)	(cont.)		(cont.)		(cont.)
10								WORDS &
								MUSIC
11								
12								
1/71								
2								
3								MEMORY GAME
4								
5								
6								
7								
8								THREE ON A
								MATCH
9								
10								
11								
12								
1/72								
2								
3								
4								
5								
6								
7								
8								
9								
10								
11								
12								
1/73								
2								
3								
4		BAFFLE						

	2:00p.m.	2:30p.m.	3:00p.m.	3:30p.m.	4:00p.m.	4:30p.m.	5:00p.m.	5:30p.m.
8	Days of Our Lives	The Doctors (cont.)	Another World	Bright Promise	Somerset (cont.)			
9	(cont.)		(cont.)	(cont.)				
10								
11								
12								
1/71								
2								
3								
4								
5								
6								
7								
8								
9								
10								
11								
12								
1/72								
2								
3								
4				RETURN TO PEYTON PLACE				
5								
6								
7								
8								
9								
10								
11								
12								
1/73								
2								
3								
4								

	10:00a.m.	10:30a.m.	11:00a.m.	11:30a.m.	12:00noon	12:30p.m.	1:00p.m.	1:30p.m.
5	Dinah's Place (cont.)	Baffle (cont.)	Sale of the Century (cont.)	Hollywood Squares (cont.)	Jeopardy (cont.)	Who, What or Where (cont.)		Three On a Match (cont.)
6								
7			WIZARD OF ODDS					
8								
9								
10								
11								
12								
1/74		Jeopardy			JACKPOT	Baffle		
2								
3								
4						CELEBRITY SWEEPSTAKES		
5								
6								
7	NAME THAT TUNE	WINNING STREAK	HIGH ROLLERS					Jeopardy
8								
9								
10								
11								
12								
1/75	Celebrity Sweepstakes	WHEEL OF FORTUNE				BLANK CHECK		How To Survive a Marriage
2								
3								
4								Days of Our Lives (to: 2:30)
5								
6								
7					MAGNIFICENT MARBLE MACHINE	Jackpot		
8								
9								
10						THREE FOR THE MONEY		
11								
12		Wheel of Fortune			High Rollers	Magnificent Marble Mach.		
1/76		High Rollers	Wheel of Fortune		Magnificent Marble Mach	TAKE MY ADVICE		

	2:00p.m.	2:30p.m.	3:00p.m.	3:30p.m.	4:00p.m.	4:30p.m.	5:00p.m.	5:30p.m.
5	Days of Our	The Doctors	Another	Return To	Somerset			
	Lives	(cont.)	World	Peyton Place	(cont.)			
6	(cont.)		(cont.)	(cont.)				
7								
8								
9								
10								
11								
12								
1/74				HOW TO				
				SURVIVE A				
2				MARRIAGE				
3								
4								
5								
6								
7								
8								
9								
10								
11								
12								
1/75			Another World					
2								
3								
4	Days of Our							
	Lives							
5	(from: 1:30)							
6								
7								
8								
9								
10								
11								
12								
1/76								

	10:00a.m.	10:30a.m.	11:00a.m.	11:30a.m.	12:00noon	12:30p.m.	1:00p.m.	1:30p.m.
2	Celebrity	High Rollers	Wheel of	Hollywood	Magnificent	Take My		Days of Our
	Sweepstakes	(cont.)	Fortune	Squares	Marble	Advice		Lives
3	(cont.)		(cont.)	(cont.)	Machine	(cont.)		(to: 2:30)
					(cont.)			(cont.)
4								
5								
6	SANFORD & SON	Celebrity			FUN FACTORY	GONG SHOW		
		Sweepstakes						
7								
8								
9								
10		Hollywood		STUMPERS	50 GRAND			
		Squares			SLAM			
11								
12								
1/77				SHOOT FOR		LOVERS AND	Gong Show	
				THE STARS		FRIENDS		
2								
3								
4					Name That			
					Tune			
5						CHICO &		
						THE MAN		
6				IT'S	Shoot For			
				ANYBODY'S	the Stars			
7				GUESS				
8								
9								
10				KNOCKOUT	TO SAY THE			
					LEAST			
11								
12						Gong Show		
1/78								
2								
3								
4	CARD SHARKS		High Rollers	Wheel of	Sanford & Son			
				Fortune				
5								
6								
7					AMERICA ALIVE			
8								
9								
10		JEOPARDY					Hollywood	
							Squares	

	2:00p.m.	2:30p.m.	3:00p.m.	3:30p.m.	4:00p.m.	4:30p.m.	5:00p.m.	5:30p.m.
2	Days of Our Lives (from: 1:30) (cont.)	The Doctors (cont.)	Another World (cont.)		Somerset (cont.)			
3								
4								
5								
6								
7								
8								
9								
10								
11								
12								
1/77								
2								
3								
4					Gong Show			
5								
6								
7								
8								
9								
10								
11								
12					FOR RICHER, FOR POORER			
1/78								
2								
3								
4								
5								
6								
7								
8								
9								
10								

	10:00a.m.	10:30a.m.	11:00a.m.	11:30a.m.	12:00noon	12:30p.m.	1:00p.m.	1:30p.m.
11	Card Sharks (cont.)	Jeopardy (cont.)	High Rollers (cont.)	Wheel of Fortune (cont.)	America Alive (cont.)		Hollywood Squares (cont.)	Days of Our Lives (to: 2:30) (cont.)
12								
1/79		ALL STAR SECRETS			Jeopardy	PASSWORD PLUS		
2								
3					Password Plus	Hollywood Squares	Days of Our Lives	
4								
5								
6								
7								
8		Hollywood Squares			MINDREADERS	Password Plus		
9								
10								
11								
12								
1/80					CHAIN REACTION			
2								
3								
4								
5								
6	DAVID LETTERMAN SHOW				Card Sharks			
7								
8	David Letterman Show		Wheel of Fortune	Password Plus			The Doctors	
9								
10	LAS VEGAS GAMBIT	BLOCKBUSTERS						
11								
12								
1/81								
2								
3								
4								
5								
6								
7								

	2:00p.m.	2:30p.m.	3:00p.m.	3:30p.m.	4:00p.m.	4:30p.m.	5:00p.m.	5:30p.m.
11	Days of Our	The Doctors	Another World (cont.)					
	Lives	(cont.)						
12	(from: 1:30)							
	(cont.)							
1/79								
2								
3	The Doctors	Another World						
4								
5								
6								
7								
8								
9								
10								
11								
12								
1/80								
2								
3								
4								
5								
6								
7								
8	Another World		TEXAS					
9								
10								
11								
12								
1/81								
2								
3								
4								
5								
6								
7								

	10:00a.m.	10:30a.m.	11:00a.m.	11:30a.m.	12:00noon	12:30p.m.	1:00p.m.	1:30p.m.
8	Las Vegas Gambit	Blockbusters (cont.)	Wheel of Fortune (cont.)	Password Plus (cont.)	Card Sharks (cont.)	The Doctors (cont.)	Days of Our Lives (cont.)	
9	(cont.)							
10				BATTLESTARS	Password Plus			
11								
12	REGIS PHILBIN SHOW							
1/82								
2								
3								
4		Wheel of Fortune	Texas			The Doctors	Search For Tomorrow	
5	DIFF'RENT STROKES							
6								
7								
8								
9								
10								
11								
12	THE FACTS OF LIFE							
1/83		SALE OF THE CENTURY	Wheel of Fortune	HIT MAN	JUST MEN			
2								
3								
4				DREAM HOUSE	Battlestars			
5								
6								
7	Diff'rent Strokes							
8					PERSONAL & CONFIDENTIAL			
9								
10					GO!			
11								
12								
1/84	The Facts of Life				HOT POTATO			
2								
3								
4								

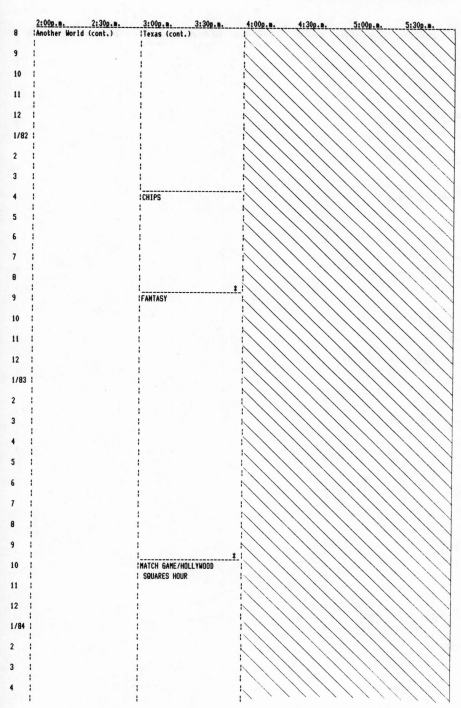

	2:00p.m.	2:30p.m.	3:00p.m.	3:30p.m.	4:00p.m.	4:30p.m.	5:00p.m.	5:30p.m.
8	Another World (cont.)		Texas (cont.)					
9								
10								
11								
12								
1/82								
2								
3								
4			CHIPS					
5								
6								
7								
8								
9			FANTASY					
10								
11								
12								
1/83								
2								
3								
4								
5								
6								
7								
8								
9								
10			MATCH GAME/HOLLYWOOD SQUARES HOUR					
11								
12								
1/84								
2								
3								
4								

	10:00a.m.	10:30a.m.	11:00a.m.	11:30a.m.	12:00noon	12:30p.m.	1:00p.m.	1:30p.m.
5	The Facts of Life (cont.)	Sale of the Century (cont.)	Wheel of Fortune (cont.)	Dream House (cont.)	Hot Potato (cont.)	Search For Tomorrow (cont.)	Days of Our Lives (cont.)	
6								
7				SCRABBLE				
8								
9								
10								
11								
12								
1/85	TIME MACHINE							
2								
3								
4								
5	The Facts of Life							
6								
7	SILVER SPOONS							
8								
9	YOUR NUMBER'S UP	BREAK THE BANK						
10								
11								
12	FAMILY TIES							
1/86								
2								
3								
4								
5								
6								
7								
8								
9		STRIKE IT RICH						
10								
11								
12								
1/87	Sale of the Century					WORD PLAY		

	2:00p.m.	2:30p.m.	3:00p.m.	3:30p.m.	4:00p.m.	4:30p.m.	5:00p.m.	5:30p.m.
5	Another World (cont.)		Match Game/Hollywood					
6			Squares Hour (cont.)					
7								
8			SANTA BARBARA					
9								
10								
11								
12								
1/85								
2								
3								
4								
5								
6								
7								
8								
9								
10								
11								
12								
1/86								
2								
3								
4								
5								
6								
7								
8								
9								
10								
11								
12								
1/87								

	10:00a.m.	10:30a.m.	11:00a.m.	11:30a.m.	12:00noon	12:30p.m.	1:00p.m.	1:30p.m.
2	Sale of the	Strike It	Wheel of	Scrabble		Word Play	Days of Our Lives (cont.)	
	Century	Rich	Fortune	(cont.)		(cont.)		
3	(cont.)	(cont.)	(cont.)					
4								
5								
6		CLASSIC						
		CONCENTRATION						
7								
8								
9				WIN, LOSE		Scrabble		
				OR DRAW				
10								
11								
12								
1/88								
2								
3								
4								
5								
6								
7								
8								
9								
10								
11								
12								
1/89								
2								
3	Scrabble					GENERATIONS		
4								
5								
6								
7			GOLDEN GIRLS					
8								

	2:00p.m.	2:30p.m.	3:00p.m.	3:30p.m.	4:00p.m.	4:30p.m.	5:00p.m.	5:30p.m.
2	Another World (cont.)		Santa Barbara (cont.)					
3								
4								
5								
6								
7								
8								
9								
10								
11								
12								
1/88								
2								
3								
4								
5								
6								
7								
8								
9								
10								
11								
12								
1/89								
2								
3								
4								
5								
6								
7								
8								

Daytime NBC
Program Moves

Date	Time	Title (Minutes) — Type	Action	From/To
9/59	10:00	Dough Re Mi (30) — QU	x	
9/59	10:30	Treasure Hunt (30) — QU	x	
9/59	11:00	The Price Is Right (30) — QU	x	
9/59	11:30	Concentration (30) — QU	x	
9/59	12:00	Tic Tac Dough (30) — QU	x	
9/59	12:30	It Could Be You (30) — QU	x	
9/59	1:00	Split Personality (30) — QU	d	
9/59	1:30	Queen for a Day (30) — TS	x	
9/59	2:30	The Thin Man (30) — CO	dp	
9/59	3:00	Young Dr. Malone (30) — SL	x	
9/59	3:30	From These Roots (30) — SL	x	
9/59	4:00	Truth or Consequences (30) — QU	x	
9/59	4:00	Truth or Consequences (30) — QU	m	To:4:30
10/59	4:00	The House on High Street (30) — SL	d	
10/59	4:30	Truth or Consequences (30) — QU	m	Fr:4
11/59	12:00	Tic Tac Dough (30) — QU	c	
11/59	4:30	Truth or Consequences (30) — QU	m	To:12
12/59	10:30	Treasure Hunt (30) — QU	c	
12/59	12:00	Truth or Consequences (30) — QU	m	Fr:4:30
1/60	10:30	Play Your Hunch (30) — QU	d	
1/60	2:30	The Thin Man (30) — CO	cp	
2/60	2:30	Loretta Young Show (30) — DA	dp	
9/60	1:00	Split Personality (30) — QU	c	
9/60	1:30	Queen for a Day (30) — TS	m	To:12:30(a)
9/60	4:00	The House on High Street (30) — SL	c	
10/60	1:00	Charge Account (30) — QU	d	
10/60	1:30	Here's Hollywood (30) — IV	d	
10/60	4:00	Make Room for Daddy (30) — SC	dp	
12/60	10:00	Dough Re Mi (30) — QU	c	
1/61	10:00	Say When (30) — QU	d	
5/61	1:00	Charge Account (30) — QU	m	To:2
6/61	2:00	Charge Account (30) — QU	m	Fr:1
12/61	12:00	Truth or Consequences (30) — QU	m	To:12:30
12/61	12:30	It Could Be You (30) — QU	c	
12/61	3:30	From These Roots (30) — SL	c	

Date	Time	Title (Minutes) — Type	Action	From/To
1/62	12:00	Your First Impression (30) — QU	d	
1/62	12:30	Truth or Consequences (30) — QU	m	Fr:12
1/62	3:30	Our Five Daughters (30) — SL	d	
9/62	2:00	Charge Account (30) — QU	c	
9/62	2:30	Loretta Young Show (30) — DA	m	To:3
9/62	3:00	Young Dr. Malone (30) — SL	m	To:3:30
9/62	3:30	Our Five Daughters (30) — SL	c	
10/62	2:00	Merv Griffin Show (60) — TK	d	
10/62	3:00	Loretta Young Show (30) — DA	m	Fr:2:30
10/62	3:30	Young Dr. Malone (30) — SL	m	Fr:3
12/62	1:30	Here's Hollywood (30) — IV	c	
12/62	4:00	Make Room for Daddy (30) — SC	m	To:4:30
1/63	4:00	Match Game (30) — QU	d	
1/63	4:30	Make Room for Daddy (30) — SC	m	Fr:4
3/63	2:00	Merv Griffin Show (60) — TK	c	
3/63	3:30	Young Dr. Malone (30) — SL	c	
4/63	2:00	Ben Jerrod (30) — SL	d	
4/63	2:30	The Doctors (30) — SL	d	
4/63	3:30	You Don't Say (30) — QU	d	
6/63	2:00	Ben Jerrod (30) — SL	c	
7/63	2:00	People Will Talk (30) — QU	d	
8/63	11:00	The Price Is Right (30) — QU	m	To:11(a)
8/63	11:30	Concentration (30) — QU	m	To:11
9/63	10:30	Play Your Hunch (30) — QU	c	
9/63	11:00	Concentration (30) — QU	m	Fr:11:30
9/63	11:30	Missing Links (30) — QU	d	
10/63	10:30	Word for Word (30) — QU	d	
12/63	2:00	People Will Talk (30) — QU	c	
1/64	2:00	Let's Make a Deal (30) — QU	d	
3/64	11:30	Missing Links (30) — QU	m	To:11:30(a)
4/64	11:30	Jeopardy (30) — QU	d	
4/64	3:00	Loretta Young Show (30) — DA	m	To:2-7/64
5/64	3:00	Another World (30) — SL	d	
6/64	10:00	Say When (30) — QU	m	To:12
6/64	12:00	Your First Impression (30) — QU	c	
6/64	2:00	Let's Make a Deal (30) — QU	m	To:1:30
6/64	4:30	Make Room for Daddy (30) — SC	m	To:10
7/64	10:00	Make Room for Daddy (30) — SC	m	Fr:4:30
7/64	12:00	Say When (30) — QU	m	Fr:10
7/64	1:30	Let's Make a Deal (30) — QU	m	Fr:2
7/64	2:00	Loretta Young Show (30) — DA	m	Fr:3-4/64
9/64	10:30	Word for Word (30) — QU	c	
10/64	10:30	What's This Song (30) — QU	d	
12/64	2:00	Loretta Young Show (30) — DA	cp	
1/65	2:00	Moment of Truth (30) — SL	d	
3/65	10:00	Make Room for Daddy (30) — SC	cp	
3/65	12:00	Say When (30) — QU	c	
3/65	12:30	Truth or Consequences (30) — QU	m	To:10
4/65	10:00	Truth or Consequences (30) — QU	m	Fr:12:30
4/65	12:00	Call My Bluff (30) — QU	d	

Date	Time	Title (Minutes) — Type	Action	From/To
4/65	12:30	I'll Bet (30) — QU	d	
8/65	10:00	Truth or Consequences (30) — QU	c	
8/65	10:30	What's This Song (30) — QU	c	
8/65	11:00	Concentration (30) — QU	m	To:10:30
8/65	11:30	Jeopardy (30) — QU	m	To:12
8/65	12:00	Call My Bluff (30) — QU	c	
8/65	12:30	I'll Bet (30) — QU	c	
9/65	10:00	Fractured Phrases (30) — QU	d	
9/65	10:30	Concentration (30) — QU	m	Fr:11
9/65	11:00	Morning Star (30) — SL	d	
9/65	11:30	Paradise Bay (30) — SL	d	
9/65	12:00	Jeopardy (30) — QU	m	Fr:11:30
9/65	12:30	Let's Play Post Office (30) — QU	d	
10/65	2:00	Moment of Truth (30) — SL	c	
11/65	2:00	Days of Our Lives (30) — SL	d	
12/65	10:00	Fractured Phrases (30) — QU	c	
1/66	10:00	Eye Guess (30) — QU	d	
7/66	11:00	Morning Star (30) — SL	c	
7/66	11:30	Paradise Bay (30) — SL	c	
7/66	12:30	Let's Play Post Office (30) — QU	c	
8/66	11:00	Chain Letter (30) — QU	d	
8/66	11:30	Showdown (30) — QU	d	
8/66	12:30	Swingin' Country (30) — MU	d	
10/66	11:00	Chain Letter (30) — QU	c	
10/66	11:30	Showdown (30) — QU	c	
11/66	11:00	Pat Boone Show (30) — TK	d	
11/66	11:30	Hollywood Squares (30) — QU	d	
12/66	10:00	Eye Guess (30) — QU	m	To:12:30
12/66	12:30	Swingin' Country (30) — MU	c	
1/67	10:00	Reach for the Stars (30) — QU	d	
1/67	12:30	Eye Guess (30) — QU	m	Fr:10
3/67	10:00	Reach for the Stars (30) — QU	c	
4/67	10:00	Snap Judgment (30) — QU	d	
6/67	11:00	Pat Boone Show (30) — TK	c	
7/67	11:00	Personality (30) — QU	d	
12/68	1:30	Let's Make a Deal (30) — QU	m	To:1:30 (a)
1/69	1:30	Hidden Faces (30) — SL	d	
3/69	10:00	Snap Judgment (30) — QU	c	
4/69	10:00	It Takes Two (30) — QU	d	
6/69	1:30	Hidden Faces (30) — SL	c	
7/69	1:30	You're Putting Me On (30) — QU	d	
9/69	11:00	Personality (30) — QU	c	
9/69	12:30	Eye Guess (30) — QU	c	
9/69	3:30	You Don't Say (30) — QU	c	
9/69	4:00	Match Game (30) — QU	c	
10/69	11:00	Sale of the Century (30) — QU	d	
10/69	12:30	Name Droppers (30) — QU	d	
10/69	3:30	Bright Promise (30) — SL	d	
10/69	4:00	Letters to Laugh-In (30) — QU	d	
12/69	12:30	Name Droppers (30) — QU	m	To:4

Date	*Time*	*Title (Minutes) — Type*	*Action*	*From/To*
12/69	1:30	You're Putting Me On (30) — QU	c	
12/69	4:00	Letters to Laugh-In (30) — QU	c	
1/70	12:30	Who, What Or Where (30) — QU	d	
1/70	1:30	Life with Linkletter (30) — TK	d	
1/70	4:00	Name Droppers (30) — QU	m	Fr:12:30
3/70	4:00	Name Droppers (30) — QU	c	
4/70	4:00	Somerset (30) — SL	d	
7/70	10:00	It Takes Two (30) — QU	c	
8/70	10:00	Dinah's Place (30) — TK	d	
9/70	1:30	Life with Linkletter (30) — TK	c	
10/70	1:30	Words & Music (30) — QU	d	
2/71	1:30	Words & Music (30) — QU	c	
3/71	1:30	Memory Game (30) — QU	d	
7/71	1:30	Memory Game (30) — QU	c	
8/71	1:30	Three on a Match (30) — QU	d	
3/72	3:30	Bright Promise (30) — SL	c	
4/72	3:30	Return to Peyton Place (30) — SL	d	
3/73	10:30	Concentration (30) — QU	c	
4/73	10:30	Baffle (30) — QU	d	
6/73	11:00	Sale of the Century (30) — QU	c	
7/73	11:00	Wizard of Odds (30) — QU	d	
12/73	10:30	Baffle (30) — QU	m	To:12:30
12/73	12:00	Jeopardy (30) — QU	m	To:10:30
12/73	12:30	Who, What Or Where (30) — QU	c	
12/73	3:30	Return to Peyton Place (30) — SL	c	
1/74	10:30	Jeopardy (30) — QU	m	Fr:12
1/74	12:00	Jackpot (30) — QU	d	
1/74	12:30	Baffle (30) — QU	m	Fr:10:30
1/74	3:30	How to Survive a Marriage (30) — SL	d	
3/74	12:30	Baffle (30) — QU	d	
4/74	12:30	Celebrity Sweepstakes (30) — QU	d	
6/74	10:00	Dinah's Place (30) — TK	c	
6/74	10:30	Jeopardy (30) — QU	m	To:1:30
6/74	11:00	Wizard of Odds (30) — QU	c	
6/74	1:30	Three on a Match (30) — QU	c	
7/74	10:00	Name That Tune (30) — QU	d	
7/74	10:30	Winning Streak (30) — QU	d	
7/74	11:00	High Rollers (30) — QU	d	
7/74	1:30	Jeopardy (30) — QU	m	Fr:10:30
12/74	10:00	Name That Tune (30) — QU	m	To:12-4/77
12/74	10:30	Winning Streak (30) — QU	c	
12/74	12:30	Celebrity Sweepstakes (30) — QU	m	To:10
12/74	1:30	Jeopardy (30) — QU	c	
12/74	3:00	Another World (30) — SL	m	To:3(60min)
12/74	3:30	How to Survive a Marriage (30) — SL	m	To:1:30
1/75	10:00	Celebrity Sweepstakes (30) — QU	m	Fr:12:30
1/75	10:30	Wheel of Fortune (30) — QU	d	
1/75	12:30	Blank Check (30) — QU	d	
1/75	1:30	How to Survive a Marriage (30) — SL	m	Fr:3:30
1/75	3:00	Another World (60) — SL	m	Fr:3(30min)

Date	*Time*	*Title (Minutes) — Type*	*Action*	*From/To*
3/75	1:30	How to Survive a Marriage (30) — SL	c	
3/75	2:00	Days of Our Lives (30) — SL	m	To:1:30
4/75	1:30	Days of Our Lives (60) — SL	m	Fr:2
6/75	12:00	Jackpot (30) — QU	m	To:12:30
6/75	12:30	Blank Check (30) — QU	c	
7/75	12:00	Magnificent Marble Machine (30) — QU	d	
7/75	12:30	Jackpot (30) — QU	m	Fr:12
9/75	12:30	Jackpot (30) — QU	c	
10/75	12:30	Three for the Money (30) — QU	d	
11/75	10:30	Wheel of Fortune (30) — QU	m	To:10:30(60min)
11/75	11:00	High Rollers (30) — QU	m	To:12
11/75	12:00	Magnificent Marble Machine (30) — QU	m	To:12:30
11/75	12:30	Three for the Money (30) — QU	c	
12/75	10:30	Wheel of Fortune (60) — QU	m	Fr:10:30(30min)
12/75	10:30	Wheel of Fortune (60) — QU	m	To:11
12/75	12:00	High Rollers (30) — QU	m	Fr:11
12/75	12:00	High Rollers (30) — QU	m	To:10:30
12/75	12:30	Magnificent Marble Machine (30) — QU	m	Fr:12
12/75	12:30	Magnificent Marble Machine (30) — QU	m	To:12
1/76	10:30	High Rollers (30) — QU	m	Fr:12
1/76	11:00	Wheel of Fortune (30) — QU	m	Fr:10:30
1/76	12:00	Magnificent Marble Machine (30) — QU	m	Fr:12:30
1/76	12:30	Take My Advice (30) — DS	d	
5/76	10:00	Celebrity Sweepstakes (30) — QU	m	To:10:30
5/76	10:30	High Rollers (30) — QU	m	To:11-4/78
5/76	12:00	Magnificent Marble Machine (30) — QU	c	
5/76	12:30	Take My Advice (30) — DS	c	
6/76	10:00	Sanford & Son (30) — SC	dp	
6/76	10:30	Celebrity Sweepstakes (30) — QU	m	Fr:10
6/76	12:00	Fun Factory (30) — QU	d	
6/76	12:30	Gong Show (30) — QU	d	
9/76	10:30	Celebrity Sweepstakes (30) — QU	c	
9/76	11:30	Hollywood Squares (30) — QU	m	To:10:30
9/76	12:00	Fun Factory (30) — QU	c	
10/76	10:30	Hollywood Squares (30) — QU	m	Fr:11:30
10/76	11:30	Stumpers (30) — QU	d	
10/76	12:00	50 Grand Slam (30) — QU	d	
12/76	11:30	Stumpers (30) — QU	c	
12/76	12:00	50 Grand Slam (30) — QU	c	
12/76	12:30	Gong Show (30) — QU	m	To:1
12/76	4:00	Somerset (30) — SL	c	
1/77	11:30	Shoot for the Stars (30) — QU	d	
1/77	12:30	Lovers and Friends (30) — SL	d	
1/77	1:00	Gong Show (30) — QU	m	Fr:12:30

Date	Time	Title (Minutes) — Type	Action	From/To
3/77	1:00	Gong Show (30) — QU	m	To:4
4/77	12:00	Name That Tune (30) — QU	m	Fr:10-12/74
4/77	12:30	Lovers and Friends (30) — SL	c	
4/77	4:00	Gong Show (30) — QU	m	Fr:1
5/77	11:30	Shoot for the Stars (30) — QU	m	To:12
5/77	12:00	Name That Tune (30) — QU	c	
5/77	12:30	Chico & the Man (30) — SC	dp	
6/77	11:30	It's Anybody's Guess (30) — QU	d	
6/77	12:00	Shoot for the Stars (30) — QU	m	Fr:11:30
9/77	11:30	It's Anybody's Guess (30) — QU	c	
9/77	12:00	Shoot for the Stars (30) — QU	c	
10/77	11:30	Knockout (30) — QU	d	
10/77	12:00	To Say the Least (30) — QU	d	
11/77	12:30	Chico & the Man (30) — SC	cp	
11/77	4:00	Gong Show (30) — QU	m	To:12:30
12/77	12:30	Gong Show (30) — QU	m	Fr:4
12/77	4:00	For Richer, For Poorer (30) — SL	d	
3/78	10:00	Sanford & Son (30) — SC	m	To:12
3/78	11:00	Wheel of Fortune (30) — QU	m	To:11:30
3/78	11:30	Knockout (30) — QU	c	
3/78	12:00	To Say the Least (30) — QU	c	
4/78	10:00	Card Sharks (30) — QU	d	
4/78	11:00	High Rollers (30) — QU	m	Fr:10:30-5/76
4/78	11:30	Wheel of Fortune (30) — QU	m	Fr:11
4/78	12:00	Sanford & Son (30) — SC	m	Fr:10
6/78	12:00	Sanford & Son (30) — SC	cp	
6/78	12:30	Gong Show (30) — QU	c	
7/78	12:00	America Alive (60) — MG	d	
9/78	10:30	Hollywood Squares (30) — QU	m	To:1
9/78	4:00	For Richer, For Poorer (30) — SL	c	
10/78	10:30	Jeopardy (30) — QU	d	
10/78	1:00	Hollywood Squares (30) — QU	m	Fr:10:30
12/78	10:30	Jeopardy (30) — QU	m	To:12
12/78	12:00	America Alive (60) — MG	c	
1/79	10:30	All Star Secrets (30) — QU	d	
1/79	12:00	Jeopardy (30) — QU	m	Fr:10:30
1/79	12:30	Password Plus (30) — QU	d	
2/79	12:00	Jeopardy (30) — QU	c	
2/79	12:30	Password Plus (30) — QU	m	To:12
2/79	1:00	Hollywood Squares (30) — QU	m	To:12:30
2/79	1:30	Days of Our Lives (60) — SL	m	To:1
2/79	2:30	The Doctors (30) — SL	m	To:2
2/79	3:00	Another World (60) — SL	m	To:2:30
3/79	12:00	Password Plus (30) — QU	m	Fr:12:30
3/79	12:30	Hollywood Squares (30) — QU	m	Fr:1
3/79	1:00	Days of Our Lives (60) — SL	m#	Fr:1:30
3/79	2:00	The Doctors (30) — SL	m	Fr:2:30
3/79	2:30	Another World (90) — SL	m	Fr:3
7/79	10:30	All Star Secrets (30) — QU	c	
7/79	12:00	Password Plus (30) — QU	m	To:12:30

Date	Time	Title (Minutes)—Type	Action	From/To
7/79	12:30	Hollywood Squares (30)—QU	m	To:10:30
8/79	10:30	Hollywood Squares (30)—QU	m	Fr:12:30
8/79	12:00	Mindreaders (30)—QU	d	
8/79	12:30	Password Plus (30)—QU	m	Fr:12
12/79	12:00	Mindreaders (30)—QU	c	
1/80	12:00	Chain Reaction (30)—QU	d	
5/80	10:00	Card Sharks (30)—QU	m	To:12
5/80	10:30	Hollywood Squares (30)—QU	c	
5/80	11:00	High Rollers (30)—QU	c	
5/80	12:00	Chain Reaction (30)—QU	c	
6/80	10:00	David Letterman Show (90)—TK	d	
6/80	12:00	Card Sharks (30)—QU	m	Fr:10
7/80	10:00	David Letterman Show (90)—TK	m	To:10(60min)
7/80	11:30	Wheel of Fortune (30)—QU	m	To:11
7/80	12:30	Password Plus (30)—QU	m	To:11:30
7/80	2:00	The Doctors (30)—SL	m	To:12:30
7/80	2:30	Another World (90)—SL	m	To:2
8/80	10:00	David Letterman Show (60)—TK	m	Fr:10(90min)
8/80	11:00	Wheel of Fortune (30)—QU	m	Fr:11:30
8/80	11:30	Password Plus (30)—QU	m	Fr:12:30
8/80	12:30	The Doctors (30)—SL	m	Fr:2
8/80	2:00	Another World (60)—SL	m#	Fr:2:30
8/80	3:00	Texas (60)—SL	d	
9/80	10:00	David Letterman Show (60)—TK	c	
10/80	10:00	Las Vegas Gambit (30)—QU	d	
10/80	10:30	Blockbusters (30)—QU	d	
9/81	11:30	Password Plus (30)—QU	m	To:12
9/81	12:00	Card Sharks (30)—QU	c	
10/81	11:30	Battlestars (30)—QU	d	
10/81	12:00	Password Plus (30)—QU	m	Fr:11:30
11/81	10:00	Las Vegas Gambit (30)—QU	c	
12/81	10:00	Regis Philbin Show (30)—TK	d	
3/82	10:30	Blockbusters (30)—QU	c	
3/82	11:00	Wheel of Fortune (30)—QU	m	To:10:30
3/82	11:30	Battlestars (30)—QU	m	To:12-4/83
3/82	12:00	Password Plus (30)—QU	c	
3/82	12:30	The Doctors (30)—SL	m	To:12
3/82	3:00	Texas (60)—SL	m	To:11
4/82	10:00	Regis Philbin Show (30)—TK	c	
4/82	10:30	Wheel of Fortune (30)—QU	m	Fr:11
4/82	11:00	Texas (60)—SL	m	Fr:3
4/82	12:00	The Doctors (30)—SL	m	Fr:12:30
4/82	12:30	Search for Tomorrow (30)—SL	m	Fr:2:30(c)
4/82	3:00	Chips (60)—CD	dp	
5/82	10:00	Diff'rent Strokes (30)—SC	dp	
8/82	3:00	Chips (60)—CD	cp	
9/82	3:00	Fantasy (60)—QU	d	
11/82	10:00	Diff'rent Strokes (30)—SC	m	To:10-7/83
12/82	10:00	The Facts of Life (30)—SC	dp	
12/82	10:30	Wheel of Fortune (30)—QU	m	To:11

Date	Time	Title (Minutes) — Type	Action	From/To
12/82	11:00	Texas (60) — SL	c	
12/82	12:00	The Doctors (30) — SL	c	
1/83	10:30	Sale of the Century (30) — QU	d	
1/83	11:00	Wheel of Fortune (30) — QU	m	Fr:10:30
1/83	11:30	Hit Man (30) — QU	d	
1/83	12:00	Just Men (30) — QU	d	
3/83	11:30	Hit Man (30) — QU	c	
3/83	12:00	Just Men (30) — QU	c	
4/83	11:30	Dream House (30) — QU	d	
4/83	12:00	Battlestars (30) — QU	m	Fr:11:30-3/82
6/83	10:00	The Facts of Life (30) — SC	m	To:10-1/84
7/83	10:00	Diff'rent Strokes (30) — SC	m	Fr:10-11/82
7/83	12:00	Battlestars (30) — QU	c	
8/83	12:00	Personal & Confidential (30) — MG	d	
9/83	12:00	Personal & Confidential (30) — MG	c	
9/83	3:00	Fantasy (60) — QU	c	
10/83	12:00	Go! (30) — QU	d	
10/83	3:00	Match Game/Hollywood Squares Hour (60) — QU	d	
12/83	10:00	Diff'rent Strokes (30) — SC	cp	
12/83	12:00	Go! (30) — QU	c	
1/84	10:00	The Facts of Life (30) — SC	m	Fr:10-6/83
1/84	12:00	Hot Potato (30) — QU	d	
6/84	11:30	Dream House (30) — QU	c	
6/84	12:00	Hot Potato (30) — QU	c	
7/84	11:30	Scrabble (30) — QU	d	
7/84	3:00	Match Game/Hollywood Squares Hour (60) — QU	c	
8/84	3:00	Santa Barbara (60) — SL	d#	
12/84	10:00	The Facts of Life (30) — SC	m	To:10-5/85
1/85	10:00	Time Machine (30) — QU	d	
4/85	10:00	Time Machine (30) — QU	c	
5/85	10:00	The Facts of Life (30) — SC	m	Fr:10-12/84
6/85	10:00	The Facts of Life (30) — SC	cp	
7/85	10:00	Silver Spoons (30) — SC	dp	
8/85	10:00	Silver Spoons (30) — SC	cp	
8/85	10:30	Sale of the Century (30) — QU	m	To:10-1/87
9/85	10:00	Your Number's Up (30) — QU	d	
9/85	10:30	Break the Bank (30) — QU	d	
11/85	10:00	Your Number's Up (30) — QU	c	
12/85	10:00	Family Ties (30) — SC	dp	
8/86	10:30	Break the Bank (30) — QU	c	
9/86	10:30	Strike It Rich (30) — QU	d	
12/86	10:00	Family Ties (30) — SC	cp	
12/86	12:30	Search for Tomorrow (30) — SL	c	
1/87	10:00	Sale of the Century (30) — QU	m	Fr:10:30-8/85
1/87	12:30	Word Play (30) — QU	d	
5/87	10:30	Strike It Rich (30) — QU	c	
6/87	10:30	Classic Concentration (30) — QU	d#	
8/87	11:30	Scrabble (30) — QU	m	To:12:30

Date	Time	Title (Minutes)—Type	Action	From/To
8/87	12:30	Word Play (30)—QU	c	
9/87	11:30	Win, Lose or Draw (30)—QU	d#	
9/87	12:30	Scrabble (30)—QU	m	Fr:11:30
2/89	10:00	Sale of the Century (30)—QU	c	
2/89	12:30	Scrabble (30)—QU	m	To:10
3/89	10:00	Scrabble (30)—QU	m#	Fr:12:30
3/89	12:30	Generations (30)—SL	d#	
6/89	11:00	Wheel of Fortune (30)—QU	m	To:10:30(c)
7/89	11:00	Golden Girls (30)—SC	dp#	

Daytime NBC
Programming Moves Summary

1959–60

Series Premieres: The House on High Street; The Loretta Young Show; Play Your Hunch; Split Personality; The Thin Man. *Key Programming Moves:* PLAY YOUR HUNCH debuted in the 10:30–11 a.m. slot in February, where it stayed for the next four years. TRUTH OR CONSEQUENCES was repeatedly moved, ending up in the 12–12:30 p.m. slot in December. Reruns of prime time's THE THIN MAN were aired in the 2:30–3 p.m. slot; they didn't fare very well (CBS' ART LINKLETTER'S HOUSE PARTY dominated the time slot) and were replaced with reruns of prime time's THE LORETTA YOUNG SHOW in February, which fared slightly better. TIC TAC DOUGH was cancelled in November, and TREASURE HUNT was cancelled one month later. At the end of the season, QUEEN FOR A DAY left NBC and was picked up by ABC, where it would run for another four years.

1960–61

Series Premieres: Charge Account; Here's Hollywood; Make Room for Daddy; Say When. *Key Programming Moves:* DOUGH RE MI was cancelled in December; SAY WHEN, a new quiz show, replaced it in the 10–10:30 a.m. slot, and occupied this slot until June 1964. CHARGE ACCOUNT, with Jan Murray, debuted in the 1–1:30 p.m. slot; in June it is moved into the 2–2:30 p.m. slot, as NBC stopped programming the 1–1:30 p.m. slot. HERE'S HOLLYWOOD, an interview program, debuted in the 1:30–2 p.m. slot, which it occupied until its cancellation in December 1962. Reruns of prime-time's THE DANNY THOMAS SHOW began airing in the 4–4:30 p.m. slot under the title MAKE ROOM FOR DADDY.

1961–62

Series Premieres: Our Five Daughters; Your First Impression. *Key Programming Moves:* In January, following the cancellation of the long-running IT COULD BE YOU, TRUTH OR CONSEQUENCES was moved into the 12:30–1 p.m. slot, which it occupied until March 1965. CHARGE ACCOUNT was cancelled at the end of the season.

1962–63

Series Premieres: Ben Jerrod; The Doctors; The Match Game; The Merv Griffin Show; People Will Talk; You Don't Say. *Key Programming Moves:* NBC tried the talk show format in daytime with THE MERV GRIFFIN SHOW; it didn't fare too well and was cancelled in less than six months. THE MATCH GAME debuted in January in the 4–4:30 p.m. slot, which it occupied for the next six years. YOUNG DR. MALONE was cancelled in March. Two other long-running series made their debuts during this season; THE DOCTORS (19 years) and YOU DON'T SAY (6 years) began their runs in April. At the end of the season, THE PRICE IS RIGHT moved to ABC.

1963–64

Series Premieres: Another World; Jeopardy; Let's Make a Deal; Missing Links; Word for Word. *Key Programming Moves:* CONCENTRATION was moved into the 11–11:30 a.m. slot, after more than five years in the 11:30–12 noon slot. SAY WHEN and YOUR FIRST IMPRESSION were cancelled in June. Two long running and highly successful quiz programs made their debuts during this season, LET'S MAKE A DEAL in January and JEOPARDY in April. ANOTHER WORLD debuted in May, beginning a 25 year run which was still going strong at the end of the 1988–89 season. In June, NBC ceased programming in the 4:30–5 p.m. slot.

1964–65

Series Premieres: Call My Bluff; I'll Bet; Moment of Truth; What's This Song. *Key Programming Moves:* Four mainstays of NBC's daytime lineup were cancelled during this season; THE LORETTA YOUNG SHOW was cancelled in December, MAKE ROOM FOR DADDY and SAY WHEN were cancelled in March, and TRUTH OR CONSEQUENCES was cancelled at the end of the season.

1965-66

Series Premieres: Chain Letter; Days of Our Lives; Eye Guess; Fractured Phrases; Let's Play Post Office; Morning Star; Paradise Bay; Showdown; Swingin' Country. *Key Programming Moves:* Going against history and conventional wisdom that says soap operas don't perform well before noon, NBC tried two new soaps between 11 a.m. and 12 noon; MORNING STAR and PARADISE BAY did not defy the odds, and both were cancelled by the summer. Despite the failure of MORNING STAR and PARADISE BAY, one of NBC's most successful soap operas made its debut during this season; ONE LIFE TO LIVE premiered in November in the 2-2:30 p.m. slot, beginning a 24 year run that was still going strong as the 1988-89 season ended.

1966-67

Series Premieres: Hollywood Squares; The Pat Boone Show; Personality; Reach for the Stars; Snap Judgment. *Key Programming Moves:* HOLLYWOOD SQUARES debuted; this very successful quiz program stayed a part of NBC's daytime schedule until May 1980.

1967-68

Key Programming Moves: NBC's daytime schedule remained completely intact for the entire season — no debuts, cancellations, or time slot changes.

1968-69

Series Premieres: Hidden Faces; It Takes Two; You're Putting Me On. *Key Programming Moves:* LET'S MAKE A DEAL departed NBC's daytime schedule, as it was picked up by ABC in January. Five of NBC's long-running quiz programs were cancelled by the end of the season — SNAP JUDGMENT, PERSONALITY, EYE GUESS, YOU DON'T SAY and THE MATCH GAME.

1969-70

Series premieres: Bright Promise; Letters to Laugh-In; Life with Linkletter; Name Droppers; Sale of the Century; Somerset; Who, What or Where. *Key Programming Moves:* SALE OF THE CENTURY debuted in the

11–11:30 a.m. slot, which it occupied until June 1973. NBC brought Art Linkletter back to daytime television in LIFE WITH LINKLETTER; it was cancelled at the end of the season. SOMERSET debuted; this soap opera was a spin-off from the successful soap ANOTHER WORLD. It became a modest hit, lasting until December 1976.

1970–71

Series Premieres: Dinah's Place; The Memory Game; Words & Music. *Key Programming Moves:* DINAH'S PLACE debuted in the 10–10:30 a.m. lead-off slot; this talk series performed well for NBC, lasting until June 1974.

1971–72

Series Premieres: Return to Peyton Place; Three on a Match. *Key Programming Moves:* THREE ON A MATCH debuted in the 1:30–2 p.m. slot; NBC had trouble finding a series that worked in this slot ever since they lost LET'S MAKE A DEAL at the end of 1968; THREE ON A MATCH provided stability in the 1:30–2 p.m. slot, lasting over two years. NBC offered a new soap opera, RETURN TO PEYTON PLACE, a spin-off from the successful prime-time serial, in April. It did not perform as expected; it was cancelled less than two years after its debut.

1972–73

Series Premieres: Baffle; Wizard of Odds. *Key Programming Moves:* Two of NBC's long-running quiz shows were cancelled during this season, CONCENTRATION in March and SALE OF THE CENTURY in June.

1973–74

Series Premieres: Celebrity Sweepstakes; High Rollers; How to Survive a Marriage; Jackpot; Name That Tune; Winning Streak. *Key Programming Moves:* DINAH'S PLACE and THREE ON A MATCH were cancelled in June. HIGH ROLLERS debuted in July.

1974–75

Series Premieres: Blank Check; The Magnificent Marble Machine; Wheel of Fortune. *Key Programming Moves:* JEOPARDY was cancelled in December. WHEEL OF FORTUNE debuted in January; this series became one of the most successful quiz shows in the history of television. In January, ANOTHER WORLD expanded to 60 minutes. In April, DAYS OF OUR LIVES expanded to 60 minutes.

1975–76

Series Premieres: The Fun Factory; The Gong Show; Sanford & Son; Take My Advice; Three for the Money. *Key Programming Moves:* THE GONG SHOW debuted in June; this series combined elements of the talent contests of earlier years and quiz programs. It was chided by critics but loved by audiences.

1976–77

Series Premieres: Chico & the Man; 50 Grand Slam; It's Anybody's Guess; Lovers and Friends; Shoot for the Stars; Stumpers. *Key Programming Moves:* NBC's morning lineup was in disarray, constantly undergoing changes during the season. SOMERSET was cancelled in December.

1977–78

Series Premieres: America Alive; Card Sharks; For Richer, For Poorer; Knockout; To Say the Least. *Key Programming Moves:* THE GONG SHOW was cancelled in June. AMERICA ALIVE debuted in July; this live, hour-long magazine program was an ambitious attempt but was not very successful. It was cancelled in less than six months.

1978–79

Series Premieres: All Star Secrets; Jeopardy; Mindreaders; Password Plus. *Key Programming Moves:* NBC offered new versions of two once-successful quiz programs, JEOPARDY and PASSWORD PLUS. JEOPARDY was cancelled in five months; PASSWORD PLUS lasted for almost three years. In March, ANOTHER WORLD expanded to 90 minutes.

1979-80

Series Premieres: Chain Reaction; The David Letterman Show. *Key Programming Moves:* Two of NBC's long-running quiz shows, HOLLY-WOOD SQUARES and HIGH ROLLERS were cancelled in May. THE DAVID LETTERMAN SHOW debuted in June; a 90-minute talk program, it did not perform as well as expected and was cut back to one hour in August. It was ultimately cancelled at the end of the season.

1980-81

Series Premieres: Blockbusters; Las Vegas Gambit; Texas. *Key Programming Moves:* ANOTHER WORLD was cut back to one hour. TEXAS debuted; this one hour-long soap opera was an attempt to play off of the success of CBS' prime-time soap DALLAS. Probably due to being scheduled opposite ABC's highly rated GENERAL HOSPITAL, TEXAS never really caught on with the audience.

1981-82

Series Premieres: Battlestars; Chips; Diff'rent Strokes; The Regis Philbin Show. *Key Programming Moves:* PASSWORD PLUS was cancelled in March. After 31 years on CBS, SEARCH FOR TOMORROW was picked up by NBC in April. Also in April, TEXAS was moved out of GENERAL HOSPI-TAL's shadow and into the 11 a.m.–12 noon slot; it still did not catch on and was cancelled in less than a year.

1982-83

Series Premieres: Dream House; The Facts of Life; Fantasy; Hit Man; Just Men; Personal & Confidential; Sale of the Century. *Key Programming Moves:* After 20 years on NBC, THE DOCTORS was cancelled in December. NBC's morning schedule was constantly changing. It kept trying new programs in an effort to find the right lineup; nothing seemed to catch on.

1983–84

Series Premieres: Go; Hot Potato; The Match Game/Hollywood Squares Hour; Scrabble. *Key Programming Moves:* NBC's morning schedule was still in disarray. SCRABBLE debuted in July; this series was still part of NBC's schedule at the end of the 1988–89 season.

1984–85

Series Premieres: Santa Barbara; Silver Spoons; Time Machine. *Key Programming Moves:* NBC's morning schedule was beginning to stabilize. SANTA BARBARA debuted in the 3–4 p.m. slot, opposite ABC's GENERAL HOSPITAL; though starting slowly, SANTA BARBARA gradually attracted an audience and became very successful for NBC.

1985–86

Series Premieres: Break the Bank; Family Ties; Your Number's Up. *Key Programming Moves:* In December, NBC began airing reruns of its prime-time hit FAMILY TIES.

1986–87

Series Premieres: Classic Concentration; Strike It Rich; Word Play. *Key Programming Moves:* NBC introduced a remake of one of its most successful quiz show; CLASSIC CONCENTRATION debuted in June. It performed better than expected.

1987–88

Series Premieres: Win, Lose or Draw. *Key Programming Moves:* WIN, LOSE OR DRAW debuted; this quiz program became a modest hit for NBC.

1988–89

Series Premieres: Generations; Golden Girls. *Key Programming Moves:* NBC lost the highly successful WHEEL OF THE FORTUNE to CBS; it replaced it with reruns of the prime-time series GOLDEN GIRLS. In March, NBC offered a new soap opera, GENERATIONS, in the 12:30–1 p.m. time slot.

Part Three
LATE-NIGHT PROGRAMMING

ABC Late-Night

October 1961–August 1989

	11:00p.m.	11:30p.m.	12:00midnight	12:30a.m.	1:00a.m.	1:30a.m.
10/61	NEWS					
11						
12						
1/62						
2						
3						
4						
5						
6						
7						
8						
9						
10						
11						
12						
1/63						
2						
3						
4						
5						
6						
7						
8						
9						
10						
11						
12						
1/64						
2						
3						
4						
5						

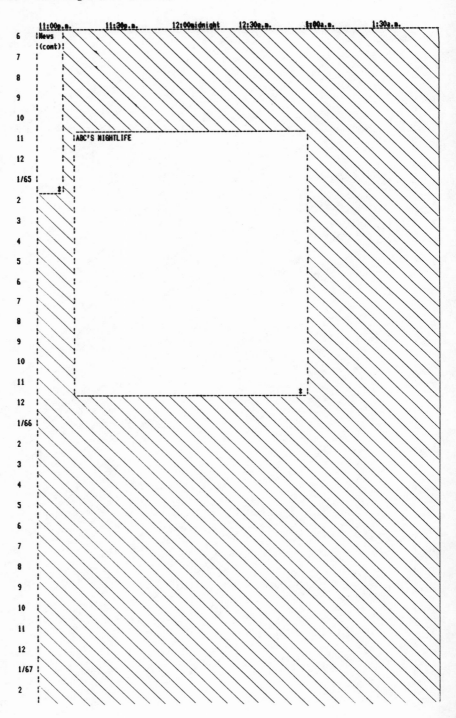

	11:00p.m.	11:30p.m.	12:00midnight	12:30a.m.	1:00a.m.	1:30a.m.
3						
4		JOEY BISHOP SHOW				
5						
6						
7						
8						
9						
10						
11						
12						
1/68						
2						
3						
4						
5						
6						
7						
8						
9						
10						
11						
12						
1/69						
2						
3						
4						
5						
6						
7						
8						
9						
10						
11						

	11:00p.m.	11:30p.m.	12:00midnight	12:30a.m.	1:00a.m.	1:30a.m.
12		Joey Bishop Show (cont.)				
		DICK CAVETT SHOW				
1/70						
2						
3						
4						
5						
6						
7						
8						
9						
10						
11						
12						
1/71						
2						
3						
4						
5						
6						
7						
8						
9						
10						
11						
12						
1/72						
2						
3						
4						
5						
6						
7						
8						

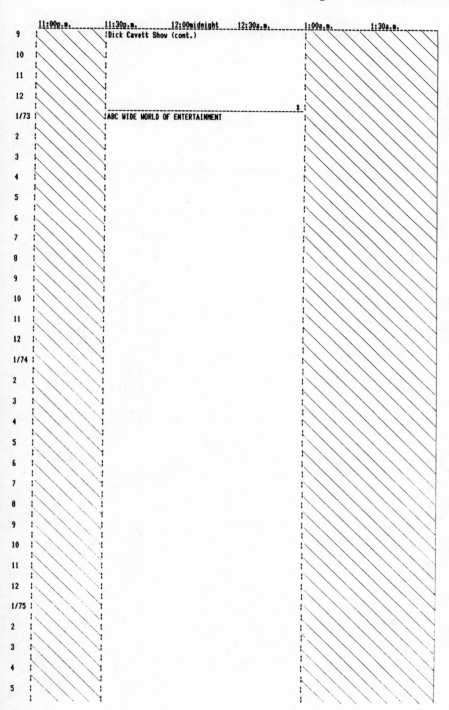

	11:00p.m.	11:30p.m.	12:00midnight	12:30a.m.	1:00a.m.	1:30a.m.
9		Dick Cavett Show (cont.)				

ABC WIDE WORLD OF ENTERTAINMENT

9
10
11
12
1/73
2
3
4
5
6
7
8
9
10
11
12
1/74
2
3
4
5
6
7
8
9
10
11
12
1/75
2
3
4
5

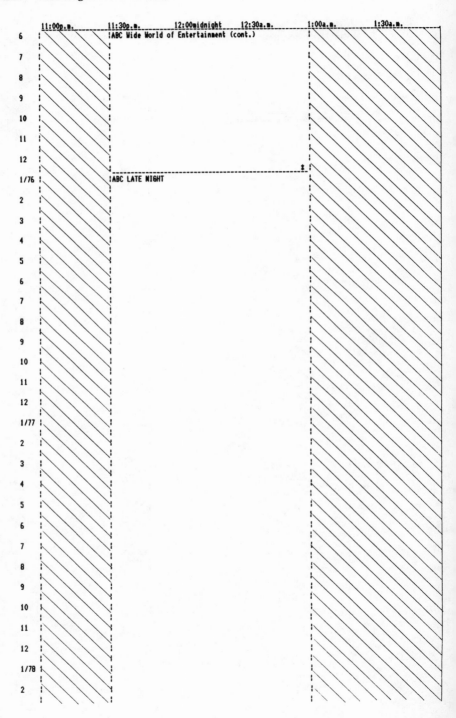

	11:00p.m.	11:30p.m.	12:00midnight	12:30a.m.	1:00a.m.	1:30a.m.
3		ABC Late Night (cont.)				

NIGHTLINE   ABC Late Night (Mon-Thur)
(Mon-Thur) (starts at 11:30 on Fridays)

3
4
5
6
7
8
9
10
11
12
1/79
2
3
4
5
6
7
8
9
10
11
12
1/80
2
3
4
5
6
7
8
9
10
11

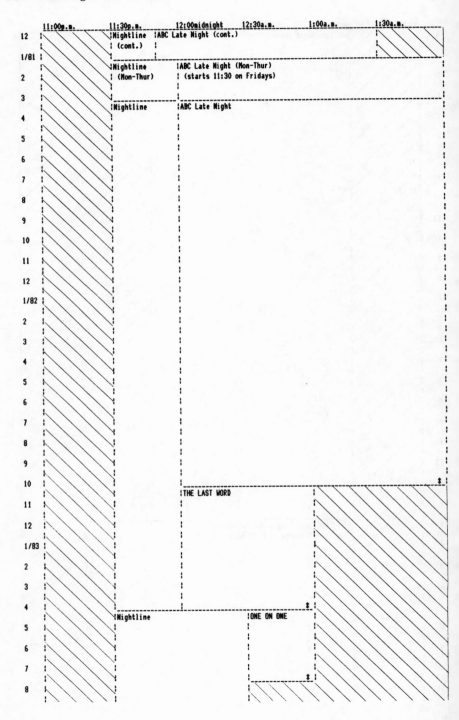

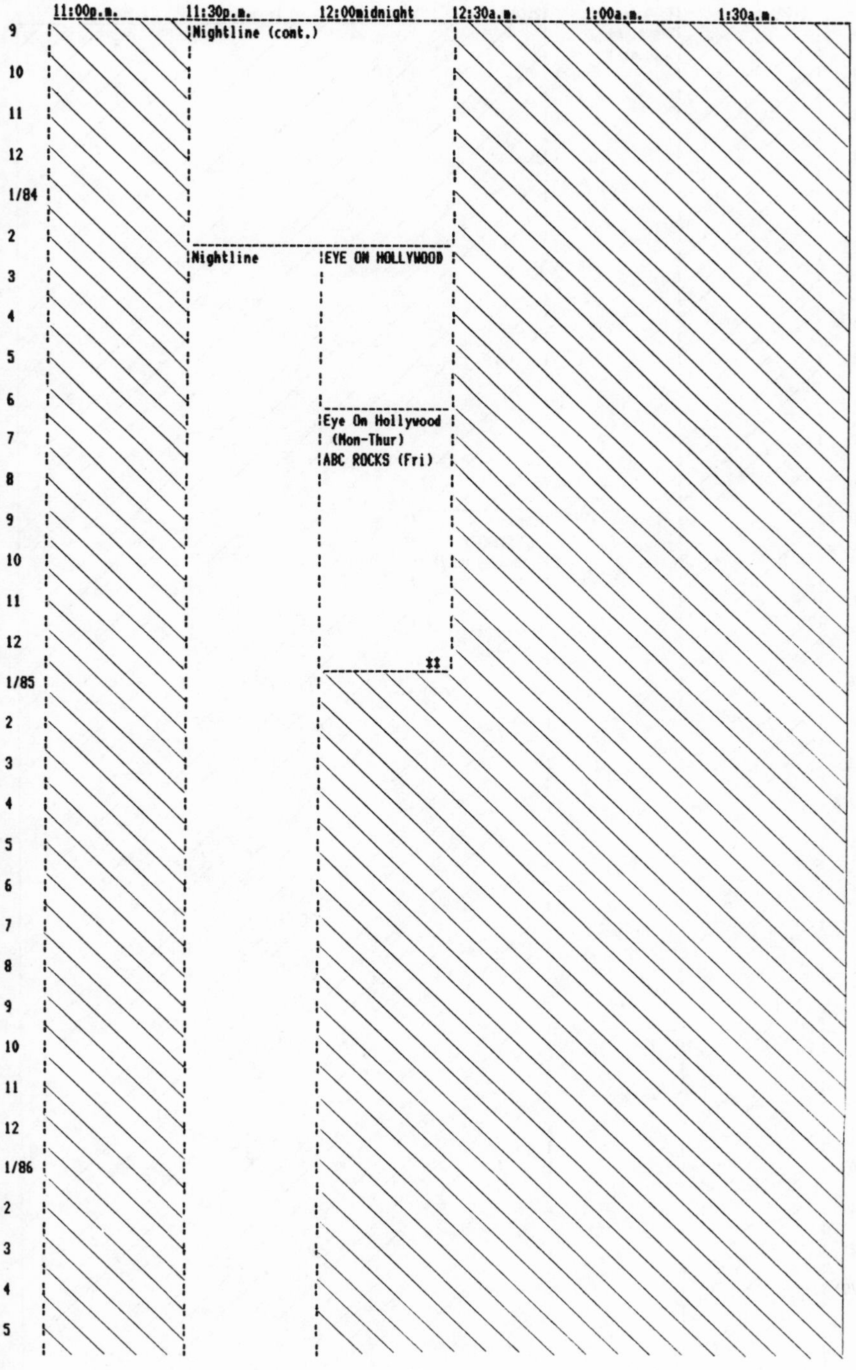

	11:00p.m.	11:30p.m.	12:00midnight	12:30a.m.	1:00a.m.	1:30a.m.

Nightline (cont.)

Nightline   EYE ON HOLLYWOOD

Eye On Hollywood
(Mon-Thur)
ABC ROCKS (Fri)

9
10
11
12
1/84
2
3
4
5
6
7
8
9
10
11
12
1/85
2
3
4
5
6
7
8
9
10
11
12
1/86
2
3
4
5

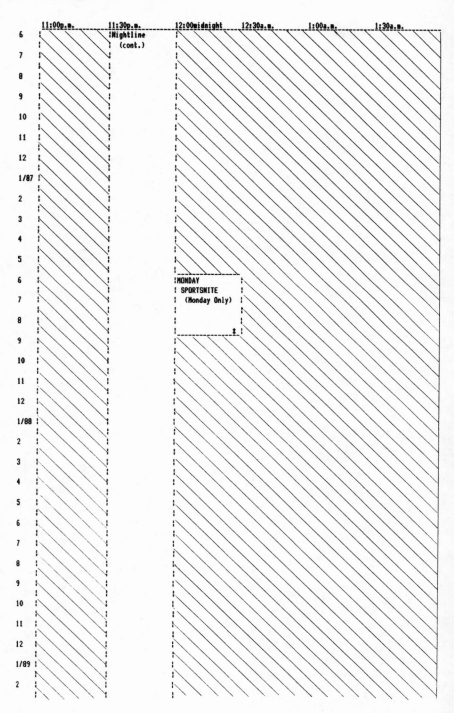

11:00p.m.   11:30p.m.   12:00midnight   12:30a.m.   1:00a.m.   1:30a.m.

Nightline
(cont.)

MONDAY
SPORTSNITE
(Monday Only)

	11:00p.m.	11:30p.m.	12:00midnight	12:30a.m.	1:00a.m.	1:30a.m.

3   Nightline
    (cont.)

4   DAY'S END

5

6

7

8

Late-Night ABC
Program Moves

Date	Time	Title (Minutes)—Type	Action	From/To
10/61	11:00	News (10)—NW	d	
11/64	11:15	ABC's Nightlife (105)—TK	d	
1/65	11:00	News (10)—NW	c	
11/65	11:15	ABC's Nightlife (105)—TK	c	
4/67	11:30	Joey Bishop Show (90)—TK	d	
12/69	11:30	Joey Bishop Show (90)—TK	c	
12/69	11:30	Dick Cavett Show (90)—TK	d	
12/72	11:30	Dick Cavett Show (90)—TK	c	
1/73	11:30	ABC Wide World of Entertainment (90)—VS	d	
12/75	11:30	ABC Wide World of Entertainment (90)—VS	c	
1/76	11:30	ABC Late Night (90)—VS	d	
2/80	11:30	ABC Late Night (90)—VS	m	To:11:50(m-r); To: 11:30(f)
3/80	11:30	Nightline (20, m-r)—NA	d	
3/80	11:50	ABC Late Night (100, m-r)—VS	m	Fr:11:50(m-f)
3/80	11:30	ABC Late Night (100, f)—VS	m	Fr:11:50(m-f)
1/81	11:30	Nightline (20, m-r)—NA	m	To:11:30(30min)
1/81	11:30	Nightline (m-r) (30)—NA	m	Fr:11:30(20min)
1/81	11:50	ABC Late Night (100, m-r)—VS	m	To:12
1/81	11:30	ABC Late Night (100, f)—VS	m	To:11:30(120min)
2/81	12:00	ABC Late Night (120, m-r)—VS	m	Fr:11:50
2/81	11:30	ABC Late Night (120, f)—VS	m	Fr:11:30(100min)
3/81	11:30	Nightline (m-r) (30)—NA	m	To:11:30(m-f)
3/81	11:30	Nightline (30)—NA	m	Fr:11:30(m-r)
3/81	12:00	ABC Late Night (120, m-r)—VS	m	To:12(m-f)
3/81	11:30	ABC Late Night (120, f)—VS	m	To:12(m-f)
4/81	12:00	ABC Late Night (120)—VS	m	Fr:12(m-r); Fr:11:30 (f)
10/82	12:00	ABC Late Night (120)—VS	c	
10/82	12:00	The Last Word (60)—NA	d	
4/83	11:30	Nightline (30)—NA	m	To:11:30(60min)
4/83	11:30	Nightline (60)—NA	m	Fr:11:30(30min)
4/83	12:00	The Last Word (60)—NA	c	

Date	Time	Title (Minutes) — Type	Action	From/To
4/83	12:30	One on One (30) — IV	d	
7/83	12:30	One on One (30) — IV	c	
2/84	11:30	Nightline (60) — NA	m	To:11:30(30min)
2/84	11:30	Nightline (30) — NA	m#	Fr:11:30(60min)
2/84	12:00	Eye on Hollywood (30) — MG	d	
6/84	12:00	Eye on Hollywood (30) — MG	m	To:12(m-r)
6/84	12:00	Eye on Hollywood (m-r) (30) — MG	m	Fr:12(m-f)
6/84	12:00	ABC Rocks (f) (30) — MU	d	
12/84	12:00	Eye on Hollywood (m-r) (30) — MG	c	
12/84	12:00	ABC Rocks (f) (30) — MU	c	
6/87	12:00	Monday Sportsnite (60, m) — TK	d	
8/87	12:00	Monday Sportsnite (60, m) — TK	c	
4/89	12:00	Day's End (60) — TK	d	
6/89	12:00	Day's End (60) — TK	c	

Programs Airing Under the Umbrella Titles:
ABC Wide World of Entertainment
ABC Late Night

1/73		ABC Late Night Special (var) (30) — VS	d	
1/73		Dick Cavett Show (90) — TK	d	
1/73		Film (var) — FI	d	
1/73		In Concert (90) — MU	d	
1/73		Jack Paar Tonight (90) — TK	d	
11/73		Jack Paar Tonight (90) — TK	c	
12/73		Wide World Mystery (90) — MA	d	
6/74		Good Night America (90) — MG	d	
9/74		Good Night America (90) — MG	c	
12/74		Dick Cavett Show (90) — TK	c	
5/75		In Concert (90) — MU	c	
9/75		ABC Late Night Special (var) (30) — VS	m	To:1/76
10/75		Longstreet (70) — CD	dp	
10/75		Mannix (70) — CD	dp	
1/76		ABC Late Night Special (var) (30) — VS	m	Fr:9/75
1/76		The Rookies (70) — CD	dp	
1/76		Wide World Mystery (90) — MA	m	To:9/76
3/76		Longstreet (70) — CD	cp	
3/76		The Magician (70) — AD	dp	
9/76		Dan August (70) — CD	dp	
9/76		The Magician (70) — AD	cp	
9/76		Mannix (70) — CD	m	To:1/79
9/76		S.W.A.T. (70) — CD	dp	
9/76		Streets of San Francisco (70) — CD	dp	
9/76		Wide World Mystery (90) — MA	m	Fr:1/76
4/77		Baretta (70) — CD	dp	
4/77		Dan August (70) — CD	cp	
4/77		Toma (70) — CD	dp	
8/77		The Rookies (70) — CD	cp	

Date	Time	Title (Minutes) — Type	Action	From/To
8/77		S.W.A.T. (70) — CD	m	To:9/78
8/77		Streets of San Francisco (70) — CD	cp	
8/77		Toma (70) — CD	m	To:1/78
8/77		Wide World Mystery (90) — MA	m	To:1/78
9/77		Police Story (70) — RA	dp	
9/77		Starsky & Hutch (70) — CD	dp	
12/77		ABC Late Night Special (var) (30) — VS	c	
1/78		Toma (70) — CD	m	Fr:8/77
1/78		Wide World Mystery (90) — MA	m	Fr:8/77
6/78		Soap (35) — SC	dp	
8/78		Police Story (70) — RA	m	To:12/78
8/78		Soap (35) — SC	m	To:4/79
8/78		Toma (70) — CD	cp	
8/78		Wide World Mystery (90) — MA	c	
9/78		Police Woman (70) — CD	dp	
9/78		S.W.A.T. (70) — CD	m	Fr:8/77
12/78		Police Story (70) — RA	m	Fr:8/78
1/79		Mannix (70) — CD	m	Fr:9/76
1/79		S.W.A.T (70) — CD	cp	
4/79		Soap (35) — SC	m	Fr:8/78
7/79		Mannix (70) — CD	cp	
8/79		Police Story (70) — RA	m	To:1/80
8/79		Soap (35) — SC	m	To:4/80
9/79		Barney Miller (35) — SC	dp	
9/79		Charlie's Angels (70) — CD	dp	
9/79		Love Boat (70) — CO	dp	
9/79		Starsky & Hutch (70) — CD	cp	
1/80		Police Story (70) — RA	m	Fr:8/79
3/80		Police Story (70) — RA	m	To:9/80
4/80		Fridays (70) — CV	d	
4/80		Soap (35) — SC	m	Fr:8/79
8/80		Baretta (70) — CD	cp	
8/80		Barney Miller (35) — SC	cp	
8/80		Soap (35) — SC	cp	
9/80		Police Story (70) — RA	m	Fr:3/80
1/81		Fantasy Island (70) — DR	dp	
1/81		Police Story (70) — RA	m	To:6/83(cbs)
2/81		Police Woman (70) — CD	cp	
3/81		Joe Forrester (70) — CD	dp	
4/81		Joe Forrester (70) — CD	cp	
9/81		Charlie's Angels (70) — CD	cp	
9/81		Film (var) — FI	m	To:1/82
10/81		Vega$ (70) — CD	dp	
1/82		Film (var) — FI	m	Fr:9/81
10/82		Fantasy Island (70) — DR	cp	
10/82		Fridays (70) — CV	c	
10/82		Love Boat (70) — CO	cp	
10/82		Film (var) — FI	c	
10/82		Vega$ (70) — CD	cp	

Late-Night ABC
Programming Moves Summary

1961–62

Key Programming Moves: ABC introduced a late-night, daily, 10-minute newscast at the beginning of the season. Ron Cochran was the regular anchor for these newscasts.

1963–64

Key Programming Moves: Murphy Martin replaced Ron Cochran as the regular anchor on ABC's late-night newscast.

1964–65

Series Premieres: ABC's Nightlife. *Key Programming Moves:* Bob Young replaced Murphy Martin as the regular anchor on ABC's late-night newscast. In November, ABC introduced ABC'S NIGHTLIFE, a 105-minute talk/interview program hosted by Les Crane, in an attempt to compete with NBC's TONIGHT SHOW STARRING JOHNNY CARSON. The program did not perform as well as ABC had hoped and was cancelled one year after it began. In January, ABC discontinued offering its daily late-night newscast.

1965–66

Key Programming Moves: ABC cancelled ABC'S NIGHTLIFE in November, after lackluster ratings.

1966–67

    Series Premieres: The Joey Bishop Show. *Key Programming Moves:* ABC made another attempt at challenging NBC's dominant position in late-night. THE JOEY BISHOP SHOW, a 90-minute talk program, debuted in April. The program started out strong; while not actually beating CARSON, it performed moderately well for ABC.

1967–68

    Key Programming Moves: The JOEY BISHOP SHOW started to slide in the ratings.

1968–69

    Key Programming Moves: THE JOEY BISHOP SHOW's ratings continued to decline.

1969–70

    Series Premieres: The Dick Cavett Show. *Key Programming Moves:* Due to declining ratings, THE JOEY BISHOP SHOW was cancelled in December. ABC replaced it with another talk program, THE DICK CAVETT SHOW. The new program regained the #2 spot in the late-night ratings race, but never really seriously challenged NBC and CARSON for #1.

1970–71

    Key Programming Moves: THE DICK CAVETT SHOW became a solid #2 in the late-night ratings behind CARSON.

1971–72

    Key Programming Moves: THE DICK CAVETT SHOW's ratings started to decline, and by the end of the season talk of cancellation had begun.

1972–73

Series Premieres: ABC Late Night Special; ABC Wide World of Entertainment; The Dick Cavett Show; In Concert; Jack Paar Tonight. *Key Programming Moves:* THE DICK CAVETT SHOW was cancelled in December. ABC replaced it with ABC WIDE WORLD OF ENTERTAINMENT, an umbrella title for a rotating menu of programs. In the beginning ABC offered ABC LATE NIGHT SPECIAL, THE DICK CAVETT SHOW, IN CONCERT and JACK PAAR TONIGHT under the umbrella.

1973–74

Series Premieres: Good Night America; Wide World Mystery. *Key Programming Moves:* During the course of the 1973–74 season, ABC made several changes under the umbrella WIDE WORLD OF ENTERTAINMENT; in November, JACK PAAR TONIGHT was cancelled; WIDE WORLD MYSTERY was added in December, and GOOD NIGHT AMERICA was added in June. GOOD NIGHT AMERICA was cancelled at the end of the season.

1974–75

Key Programming Moves: ABC cancelled THE DICK CAVETT SHOW in December and IN CONCERT in May, leaving only movies, THE ABC LATE NIGHT SPECIAL, and WIDE WORLD MYSTERY under its late-night umbrella.

1975–76

Series Premieres: ABC Late Night; Longstreet; The Magician; Mannix; The Rookies. *Key Programming Moves:* ABC added reruns of selected prime-time series to its late-night umbrella. MANNIX and LONGSTREET were introduced at the beginning of the season. In January, ABC replaced WIDE WORLD OF ENTERTAINMENT with a new umbrella title, ABC LATE NIGHT. THE ROOKIES was added in January, and THE MAGICIAN replaced LONGSTREET in March. At the end of the season, THE MAGICIAN was cancelled.

1976–77

Series Premieres: Baretta; Dan August; S.W.A.T.; The Streets of San Francisco; Toma. *Key Programming Moves:* ABC made several changes under the ABC LATE NIGHT umbrella. Reruns of THE STREETS OF SAN FRANCISCO, DAN AUGUST and S.W.A.T. were added at the beginning of the season. In April, DAN AUGUST was dropped, and reruns of TOMA and BARETTA were added. At the end of the season, THE ROOKIES and THE STREETS OF SAN FRANCISCO were dropped.

1977–78

Series Premieres: Police Story; Soap; Starsky & Hutch. *Key Programming Moves:* ABC again made several changes under its late-night umbrella. Reruns of prime-time's POLICE STORY and STARSKY & HUTCH were added to the umbrella at the beginning of the season. In December, THE ABC LATE NIGHT SPECIAL was dropped. In June, reruns of the prime-time situation comedy SOAP were added to the lineup. At the end of the season, TOMA and WIDE WORLD MYSTERY were dropped.

1978–79

Series Premieres: Police Woman. *Key Programming Moves:* Reruns of prime-time's POLICE WOMAN were added to ABC's late-night umbrella at the beginning of the season. In January, S.W.A.T. was dropped. STARSKY & HUTCH and MANNIX were dropped at the end of the season.

1979–80

Series Premieres: Barney Miller; Charlie's Angels; Fridays; The Love Boat; Nightline. *Key Programming Moves:* ABC continued to revise its late-night offerings under the umbrella ABC LATE NIGHT. Reruns of BARNEY MILLER, THE LOVE BOAT and CHARLIE'S ANGELS were added at the beginning of the season. NIGHTLINE, a 20-minute news analysis program airing Monday through Thursday, made its official debut in March. As a result of the introduction of NIGHTLINE, ABC LATE NIGHT was moved back to an 11:50 p.m. start time on Monday through Thursday. On Friday it continued to start at 11:30 p.m. At the end of the season, BARNEY MILLER, SOAP and BARETTA were dropped from the late-night schedule.

1980-81

Series Premieres: Fantasy Island; Joe Forrester. *Key Programming Moves:* ABC continued to make changes in its late-night umbrella. During the course of the season, reruns of FANTASY ISLAND and JOE FORRESTER were added. By the end of the season, POLICE WOMAN, CHARLIE'S ANGELS and JOE FORRESTER were dropped. In January, NIGHTLINE expanded to 30 minutes, still airing Monday through Thursday; consequently ABC LATE NIGHT was moved back to a 12:00 midnight start on Monday through Thursday, while remaining at 11:30 p.m. on Friday. In March, NIGHTLINE began airing five nights a week; ABC LATE NIGHT now began at 12:00 midnight five nights a week.

1981-82

Series Premieres: Vega$. *Key Programming Moves:* Reruns of VEGA$ were added to ABC's late-night lineup. At the end of the season, ABC cancelled the umbrella series ABC LATE NIGHT.

1982-83

Series Premieres: The Last Word; One on One. *Key Programming Moves:* After 10 years of the late-night umbrella concept, ABC introduced THE LAST WORD, a one-hour news analysis program. It was scheduled from 12-1 a.m., immediately following NIGHTLINE. It didn't fare too well and was cancelled in April. In April, NIGHTLINE expanded to 60 minutes, and a new interview program, ONE ON ONE, was introduced. ONE ON ONE only lasted three months before it was cancelled, leaving NIGHTLINE as ABC's sole entry in the late-night arena.

1983-84

Series Premieres: ABC Rocks; Eye on Hollywood. *Key Programming Moves:* In February, NIGHTLINE was cut back to 30 minutes, and EYE ON HOLLYWOOD debuted. EYE ON HOLLYWOOD, a 30-minute magazine program focusing on the entertainment industry, aired in the 12-12:30 a.m. slot, following NIGHTLINE. In June, EYE ON HOLLYWOOD was cut back to a Monday through Thursday schedule as ABC ROCKS debuted; airing in the 12-12:30 a.m. slot on Friday, ABC ROCKS consisted of current music videos.

1984–85

Key Programming Moves: EYE ON HOLLYWOOD and ABC ROCKS were cancelled in December, leaving NIGHTLINE as ABC's lone entry in the late-night derby.

1986–87

Series Premieres: Monday Sportsnite. *Key Programming Moves:* In June, ABC introduced MONDAY SPORTSNITE, a 30 minute sports talk show, following NIGHTLINE on Mondays. ABC cancelled the series at the end of the season.

1988–89

Series Premieres: Day's End. *Key Programming Moves:* In April, ABC introduced DAY'S END, a 60 minute talk program. It fared poorly and was cancelled by June.

CBS Late-Night

August 1969–August 1989

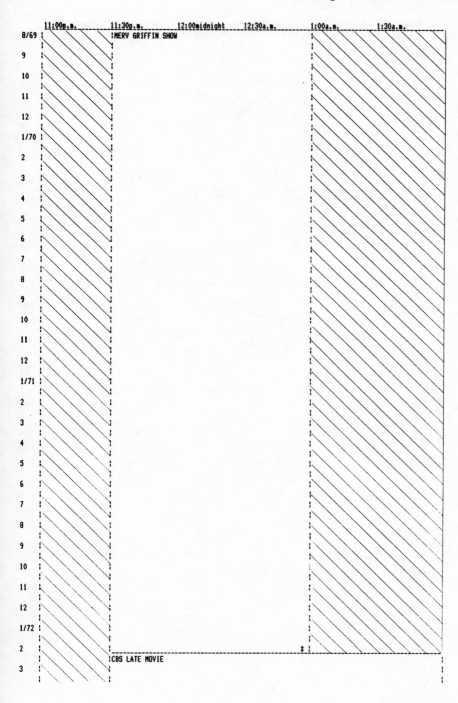

	11:00p.m.	11:30p.m.	12:00midnight	12:30a.m.	1:00a.m.	1:30a.m.
4		CBS Late Movie (cont.)				
5						
6						
7						
8						
9						
10						
11						
12						
1/73						
2						
3						
4						
5						
6						
7						
8						
9						
10						
11						
12						
1/74						
2						
3						
4						
5						
6						
7						
8						
9						
10						
11						
12						

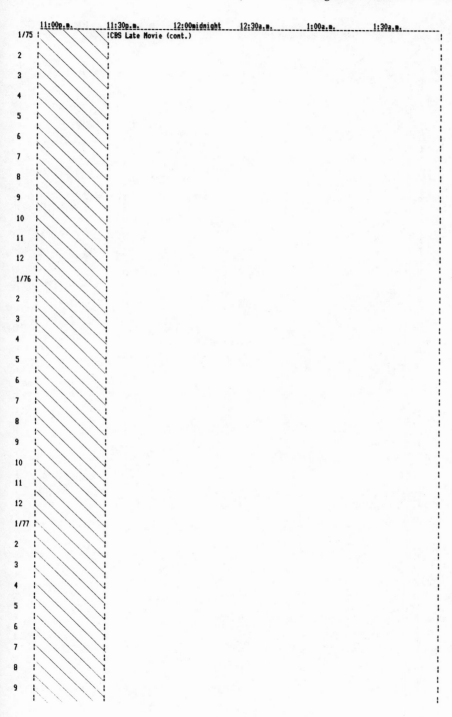

	11:00p.m.	11:30p.m.	12:00midnight	12:30a.m.	1:00a.m.	1:30a.m.
1/75		CBS Late Movie (cont.)				
2						
3						
4						
5						
6						
7						
8						
9						
10						
11						
12						
1/76						
2						
3						
4						
5						
6						
7						
8						
9						
10						
11						
12						
1/77						
2						
3						
4						
5						
6						
7						
8						
9						

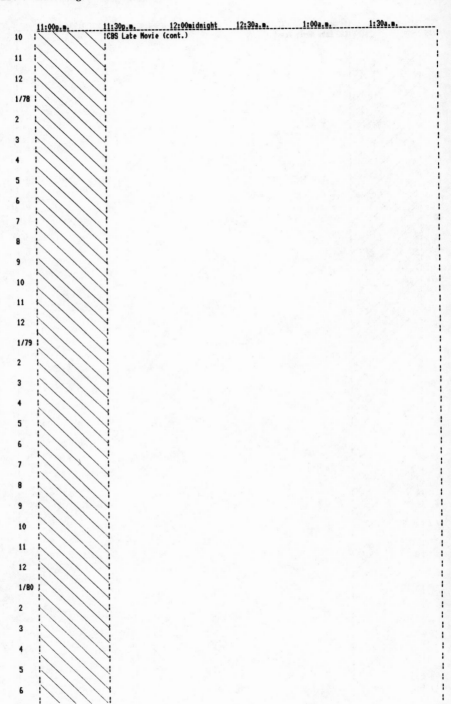

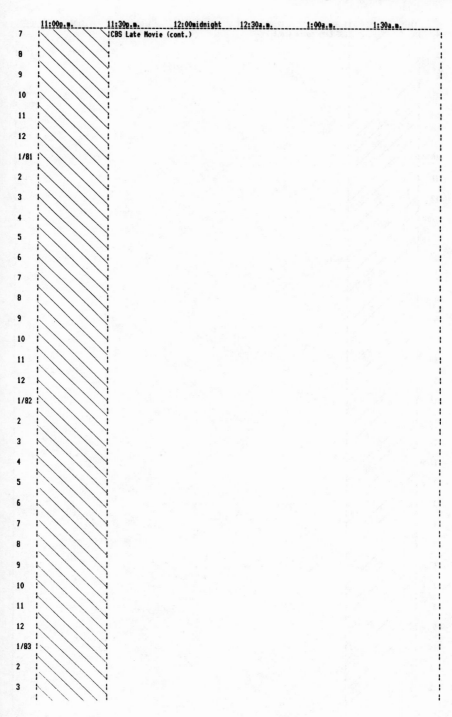

	11:00p.m.	11:30p.m.	12:00midnight	12:30a.m.	1:00a.m.	1:30a.m.
7		CBS Late Movie (cont.)				
8						
9						
10						
11						
12						
1/81						
2						
3						
4						
5						
6						
7						
8						
9						
10						
11						
12						
1/82						
2						
3						
4						
5						
6						
7						
8						
9						
10						
11						
12						
1/83						
2						
3						

	11:00p.m.	11:30p.m.	12:00midnight	12:30a.m.	1:00a.m.	1:30a.m.
4		CBS Late Movie (cont.)				
5						
6						
7						
8						
9						
10						
11						
12						
1/84						
2						
3						
4						
5						
6						
7						
8						
9						
10						
11						
12						
1/85						
2						
3						
4						
5						
6						
7						
8						
9						
10						
11						
12						

	11:00p.m.	11:30p.m.	12:00midnight	12:30a.m.	1:00a.m.	1:30a.m.
1/86		CBS Late Movie (cont.)				
2						
3						
4						
5						
6						
7						
8						
9						
10						
11						
12						
1/87						
2						
3						
4						
5						
6						
7						
8						
9						
10						
11						
12						
1/88						
2						
3						
4						
5						
6						
7						
8						
9						

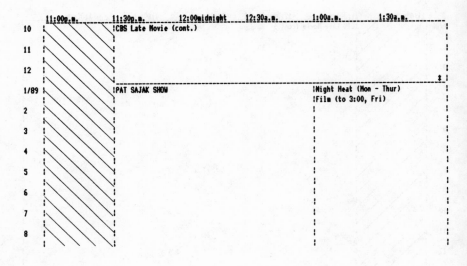

Late-Night CBS
Program Moves

Date	Time	Title (Minutes) — Type	Action	From/To
8/69	11:30	Merv Griffin Show (90) — TK	d	
2/72	11:30	Merv Griffin Show (90) — TK	c	
2/72	11:30	CBS Late Movie (150) — VS	d	
12/88	11:30	CBS Late Movie (150) — VS	c	
1/89	11:30	Pat Sajak Show (90) — TK	d#	
1/89	1:00	Night Heat (60, m-r) — CD	m#	Fr:11:30
1/89	1:00	Film (120, f) — FI	m#	Fr:11:30

Programs Airing Under the Umbrella Title:
CBS Late Movie

Date	Title (Minutes) — Type	Action	From/To
2/72	Film (var) — FI	d	
9/76	Kojak (70) — CD	dp	
9/77	M*A*S*H (35) — SC	dp	
9/77	Hawaii Five-O (70) — CD	dp	
9/78	Barnaby Jones (70) — CD	dp	
9/78	The New Avengers (70) — SD	d	
9/78	Rockford Files (70) — CD	dp	
11/78	Hawaii Five-O (70) — CD	m	To:5/79
3/79	The New Avengers (70) — SD	m	To:9/80
5/79	Hawaii Five-O (70) — CD	m	Fr:11/78
5/79	Kolchak: The Night Stalker (70) — DR	dp	
6/79	Switch (70) — CD	dp	
9/79	Baa Baa Blacksheep (70) — WD	dp	
9/79	Banacek (var) — CD	dp	
9/79	Columbo (var) — CD	dp	
9/79	Harry-O (70) — CD	dp	
9/79	Kojak (70) — CD	cp	
9/79	M*A*S*H (35) — SC	cp	
9/79	McCloud (var) — CD	dp	
9/79	McMillan & Wife (var) — CD	dp	
9/79	Madigan (var) — CD	dp	
9/79	Rockford Files (70) — CD	cp	
9/79	Switch (70) — CD	cp	

Date	Time	Title (Minutes) — Type	Action	From/To
12/79		The Avengers (70) — SD	dp	
12/79		Banacek (var) — CD	m	To:12/81
12/79		Hawaii Five-O (70) — CD	m	To:6/84
12/79		Kolchak: The Night Stalker (70) — DR	m	To:6/81
12/79		McCloud (var) — CD	m	To:9/81
12/79		McMillan & Wife (var) — CD	m	To:9/80
12/79		Madigan (var) — CD	m	To:8/81
12/79		Mary Hartman, Mary Hartman (35) — SC	d	
12/79		The Return of the Saint (70) — MY	d	
4/80		Columbo (var) — CD	m	To:3/81
5/80		The Jeffersons (35) — SC	dp	
6/80		Baa Baa Blacksheep (70) — WD	cp	
6/80		Mary Hartman, Mary Hartman (35) — SC	c	
6/80		The Return of the Saint (70) — MY	c	
7/80		Cannon (70) — CD	dp	
7/80		The Saint (70) — MY	dp	
9/80		The Avengers (70) — SD	cp	
9/80		Barnaby Jones (70) — CD	cp	
9/80		Cannon (70) — CD	m	To:8/81
9/80		Harry-O (70) — CD	m	To:3/81
9/80		Lou Grant (70) — ND	dp	
9/80		McMillan & Wife (var) — CD	m	Fr:12/79
9/80		The New Avengers (70) — SD	m	Fr:3/79
9/80		No Holds Barred (70) — CV	d	
9/80		Quincy, M.E. (70) — CD	dp	
10/80		No Holds Barred (70) — CV	c	
10/80		The Saint (70) — MY	m	To:8/81
3/81		Columbo (var) — CD	m	Fr:4/80
3/81		Harry-O (70) — CD	m	Fr:9/80
3/81		Lou Grant (70) — ND	cp	
3/81		The New Avengers (70) — SD	m	To:6/84
5/81		McMillan & Wife (var) — CD	m	To:3/82
6/81		Hec Ramsey (var) — WE	dp	
6/81		Kolchak: The Night Stalker (70) — DR	m	Fr:12/79
8/81		Cannon (70) — CD	m	Fr:9/80
8/81		Columbo (var) — CD	m	To:3/82
8/81		Hec Ramsey (var) — WE	cp	
8/81		Madigan (var) — CD	m	Fr:12/79
8/81		The Saint (70) — MY	m	Fr:10/80
9/81		Alice (35) — SC	dp	
9/81		Behind the Screen (35) — SL	d	
9/81		Cannon (70) — CD	cp	
9/81		The Jeffersons (35) — SC	cp	
9/81		Kolchak: The Night Stalker (70) — DR	m	To:10/87
9/81		McCloud (var) — CD	m	Fr:12/79

Date	Time	Title (Minutes) — Type	Action	From/To
9/81		Madigan (var) — CD	cp	
9/81		WKRP in Cincinnati (35) — SC	dp	
11/81		Harry-O (70) — CD	cp	
12/81		Banacek (var) — CD	m	Fr:12/79
1/82		Behind the Screen (35) — SL	c	
2/82		Banacek (var) — CD	cp	
2/82		The Saint (70) — MY	cp	
3/82		Columbo (var) — CD	m	Fr:8/81
3/82		McMillan & Wife (var) — CD	m	Fr:5/81
7/82		WKRP in Cincinnati (35) — SC	cp	
9/82		Alice (35) — SC	cp	
9/82		Archie Bunker's Place (35) — SC	dp	
9/82		Trapper John, MD (70) — MD	dp	
12/82		Archie Bunker's Place (35) — SC	cp	
12/82		Hart to Hart (70) — AD	dp	
6/83		Police Story (70) — RA	m	Fr:1/81(abc)
8/83		McMillan & Wife (var) — CD	m	To:9/84
8/83		Quincy, M.E. (70) — CD	cp	
9/83		Magnum, PI (70) — CD	dp	
6/84		Hawaii Five-O (70) — CD	m	Fr:12/79
6/84		The New Avengers (70) — SD	m	Fr:3/81
6/84		Police Story (70) — RA	cp	
6/84		Trapper John, MD (70) — MD	cp	
8/84		Hart to Hart (70) — AD	cp	
8/84		Hawaii Five-O (70) — CD	m	To:2/86
8/84		McCloud (var) — CD	m	To:5/85
8/84		The New Avengers (70) — SD	c	
9/84		Fall Guy (70) — AD	dp	
9/84		McMillan & Wife (var) — CD	m	Fr:8/83
9/84		Newhart (35) — SC	dp	
9/84		Simon & Simon (70) — CD	dp	
2/85		Night Heat (70) — CD	d	
4/85		McMillan & Wife (var) — CD	cp	
4/85		Newhart (35) — SC	cp	
5/85		McCloud (var) — CD	m	Fr:8/84
7/85		Columbo (var) — CD	cp	
7/85		Fall Guy (70) — AD	cp	
7/85		McCloud (var) — CD	cp	
7/85		Magnum, PI (70) — CD	m	To:2/86
9/85		Remington Steele (70) — CD	dp	
9/85		T.J. Hooker (70) — CD	dp	
2/86		Hawaii Five-O (70) — CD	m	Fr:8/84
2/86		Magnum, PI (70) — CD	m	Fr:7/85
5/86		Hawaii Five-O (70) — CD	m	To:1/87
5/86		Remington Steele (70) — CD	cp	
8/86		Magnum, PI (70) — CD	cp	
9/86		Adderly (70) — CD	d	
9/86		Hot Shots (70) — CD	d	
12/86		Hot Shots (70) — CD	m	To:7/87
1/87		Hawaii Five-O (70) — CD	m	Fr:5/86

Date	*Time*	*Title (Minutes)—Type*	*Action*	*From/To*
1/87		Keep on Cruisin' (70)—VY	d	
2/87		Hawaii Five-O (70)—CD	cp	
2/87		Keep on Cruisin' (70)—VY	c	
7/87		Hot Shots (70)—CD	m	Fr:12/86
8/87		Hot Shots (70)—CD	c	
8/87		Simon & Simon (70)—CD	cp	
8/87		T.J. Hooker (70)—CD	cp	
10/87		Diamonds (70)—CO	d	
10/87		Hunter (70)—CD	dp	
10/87		Kolchak: The Night Stalker (70)—DR	m	Fr:9/81
3/88		Kolchak: The Night Stalker (70)—DR	cp	
7/88		Adderly (70)—CD	c	
8/88		Diamonds (70)—CO	c	
12/88		Film (var)—FI	m	To:1-1/89(fri)
12/88		Hunter (70)—CD	cp	
12/88		Night Heat (70)—CD	m	To:1-1/89(m-r)

Late-Night CBS
Programming Moves Summary

1969–70

Series Premieres: The Merv Griffin Show. *Key Programming Moves:* CBS joined the late-night competition by offering its own late-night talk show; THE MERV GRIFFIN SHOW made its debut at the beginning of the 1969–70 season. It was not a serious threat to NBC's TONIGHT SHOW STARRING JOHNNY CARSON, though it did beat out THE JOEY BISHOP SHOW for second place.

1970–71

Key Programming Moves: THE MERV GRIFFIN SHOW dropped into third place in the network late-night ratings race.

1971–72

Series Premieres: The CBS Late Movie. *Key Programming Moves:* THE MERV GRIFFIN SHOW was cancelled in February. CBS replaced it with THE CBS LATE MOVIE.

1976–77

Series Premieres: Kojak. *Key Programming Moves:* Following ABC's lead, CBS added reruns of a prime-time crime drama series, KOJAK, to its late-night lineup, under the umbrella title THE CBS LATE MOVIE.

1977-78

Series Premieres: Hawaii Five-O; M*A*S*H. *Key Programming Moves:* CBS added reruns of M*A*S*H and HAWAII FIVE-O to its late-night umbrella, THE CBS LATE MOVIE.

1978-79

Series Premieres: Barnaby Jones; Kolchak: The Night Stalker; The New Avengers; The Rockford Files; Switch. *Key Programming Moves:* During the course of the 1978-79 season, CBS made several changes under its late-night umbrella. Reruns of THE ROCKFORD FILES and BARNABY JONES were added at the beginning of the season, as was THE NEW AVENGERS; reruns of KOLCHAK: THE NIGHT STALKER and SWITCH were added during the summer. At the end of the season, THE ROCKFORD FILES, M*A*S*H, KOJAK and SWITCH were dropped from CBS' late-night lineup.

1979-80

Series Premieres: The Avengers; Baa Baa Black Sheep; Banacek; Cannon; Columbo; Harry-O; The Jeffersons; McCloud; McMillan & Wife; Madigan; Mary Hartman, Mary Hartman; The Return of the Saint; The Saint. *Key Programming Moves:* CBS added over a dozen new titles (mostly reruns of prime-time series) to its late-night umbrella during the 1979-80 season. By the end of the season, MARY HARTMAN, MARY HARTMAN, BAA BAA BLACKSHEEP, THE RETURN OF THE SAINT, THE AVENGERS and BARNABY JONES were dropped from the rotation.

1980-81

Series Premieres: Hec Ramsey; Lou Grant; No Holds Barred; Quincy, M.E. *Key Programming Moves:* CBS made several changes in its late-night umbrella lineup. Reruns of the prime-time series QUINCY, M.E., LOU GRANT and HEC RAMSEY were added, as was a new comedy series, NO HOLDS BARRED. By the end of the season, the following series were dropped from the umbrella: NO HOLDS BARRED, LOU GRANT, HEC RAMSEY, THE JEFFERSONS, CANNON and MADIGAN.

1981–82

Series Premieres: Alice; Behind the Screen; WKRP in Cincinnati. *Key Programming Moves:* CBS again made several changes in its late-night umbrella lineup. Reruns of ALICE and WKRP IN CINCINNATI were added, as was BEHIND THE SCREEN, a new soap opera. By the end of the season, HARRY-O, BEHIND THE SCREEN, BANACEK, THE SAINT, WKRP IN CINCINNATI and ALICE were dropped from the lineup.

1982–83

Series Premieres: Archie Bunker's Place; Hart to Hart; Trapper John, MD. *Key Programming Moves:* Reruns of TRAPPER JOHN, MD, HART TO HART and ARCHIE BUNKER'S PLACE were added to CBS' late-night umbrella. QUINCY, M.E. and ARCHIE BUNKER'S PLACE were dropped by season's end.

1983–84

Series Premieres: Magnum, P.I. *Key Programming Moves:* Reruns of prime-time's MAGNUM, P.I. were added to the CBS late-night umbrella. POLICE STORY, TRAPPER JOHN, MD, HART TO HART and THE NEW AVENGERS were dropped by the end of the season.

1984–85

Series Premieres: The Fall Guy; Newhart; Night Heat; Simon & Simon. *Key Programming Moves:* Reruns of NEWHART, THE FALL GUY and SIMON & SIMON were added to the CBS late-night lineup at the beginning of season. In February, NIGHT HEAT, a first-run crime drama, debuted under the late-night umbrella. By season's end, MCMILLAN & WIFE, NEWHART, THE FALL GUY, McCLOUD and COLUMBO were cancelled.

1985–86

Series Premieres: Remington Steele; T.J. Hooker. *Key Programming Moves:* CBS made some minor changes in its late-night umbrella; reruns of T.J. HOOKER and REMINGTON STEELE were added. At the end of the season, MAGNUM, P.I. and REMINGTON STEELE were dropped.

1986–87

Series Premieres: Adderly; Hot Shots; Keep on Cruisin'. *Key Programming Moves:* CBS added three new first-run series to its late-night lineup: ADDERLY, HOT SHOTS and KEEP ON CRUISIN'. Two of these, HOT SHOTS and KEEP ON CRUISIN', were cancelled by season's end, as were HAWAII FIVE-O, T.J. HOOKER and SIMON & SIMON.

1987–88

Series Premieres: Diamonds; Hunter. *Key Programming Moves:* Reruns of prime-time's HUNTER and the first-run series DIAMONDS were added to CBS' late-night umbrella. By season's end, ADDERLY, DIAMONDS and KOLCHAK: THE NIGHT STALKER were dropped.

1988–89

Series Premieres: The Pat Sajak Show. *Key Programming Moves:* In December, after 15 years, CBS discontinued its late-night umbrella, THE CBS LATE MOVIE. In January, CBS attempted a head-to-head challenge to NBC and THE TONIGHT SHOW STARRING JOHNNY CARSON with a new talk show, its first in over 15 years; THE PAT SAJAK SHOW made its debut. It started out performing nicely for CBS, but by season's end, the ratings declined and the future of the program was not promising.

NBC Late-Night

September 1959–August 1989

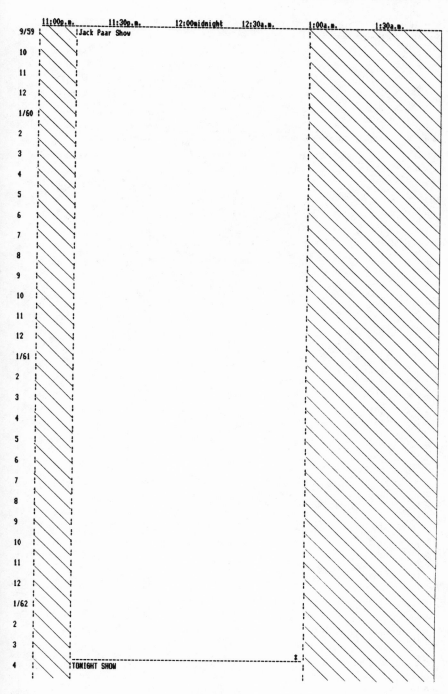

	11:00p.m.	11:30p.m.	12:00midnight	12:30a.m.	1:00a.m.	1:30a.m.
5		Tonight Show (cont.)				
6						
7						
8						
9						
10		TONIGHT SHOW STARRING JOHNNY CARSON				
11						
12						
1/63						
2						
3						
4						
5						
6						
7						
8						
9						
10						
11						
12						
1/64						
2						
3						
4						
5						
6						
7						
8						
9						
10						
11						
12						
1/65						

	11:00p.m.	11:30p.m.	12:00midnight	12:30a.m.	1:00a.m.	1:30a.m.
2		Tonight Show Starring Johnny Carson (cont.)				
3						
4						
5						
6						
7						
8						
9						
10						
11						
12						
1/66						
2						
3						
4						
5						
6						
7						
8						
9						
10						
11						
12						
1/67		Tonight Show Starring Johnny Carson				
2						
3						
4						
5						
6						
7						
8						
9						
10						

	11:00p.m.	11:30p.m.	12:00midnight	12:30a.m.	1:00a.m.	1:30a.m.
11		Tonight Show Starring Johnny Carson (cont.)				
12						
1/68						
2						
3						
4						
5						
6						
7						
8						
9						
10						
11						
12						
1/69						
2						
3						
4						
5						
6						
7						
8						
9						
10						
11						
12						
1/70						
2						
3						
4						
5						
6						
7						

	11:00p.m.	11:30p.m.	12:00midnight	12:30a.m.	1:00a.m.	1:30a.m.
8			Tonight Show Starring Johnny Carson (cont.)			

MIDNIGHT SPECIAL (to: 2:30, Fri)

	11:00p.m.	11:30p.m.	12:00midnight	12:30a.m.	1:00a.m.	1:30a.m.
5		Tonight Show Starring Johnny Carson (cont.)			Midnight Special (to: 2:30, Fri) (cont.)	
6						
7						
8						
9						
10					TOMORROW SHOW (Mon-Thur) Midnight Special (to: 2:30, Fri)	
11						
12						
1/74						
2						
3						
4						
5						
6						
7						
8						
9						
10						
11						
12						
1/75						
2						
3						
4						
5						
6						
7						
8						
9						
10						
11						
12						
1/76						

	11:00p.m.	11:30p.m.	12:00midnight	12:30a.m.	1:00a.m.	1:30a.m.
2		Tonight Show Starring Johnny Carson (cont.)			Tomorrow Show (Mon-Thur, cont.)	
3					Midnight Special (to: 2:30, Fri) (cont.)	
4						
5						
6						
7						
8						
9						
10						
11						
12						
1/77						
2						
3						
4						
5						
6						
7						
8						
9						
10						
11						
12						
1/78						
2						
3						
4						
5						
6						
7						
8						
9						
10						

	11:00p.m.	11:30p.m.	12:00midnight	12:30a.m.	1:00a.m.	1:30a.m.
11		Tonight Show Starring Johnny Carson (cont.)			Tomorrow Show (Mon-Thur, cont.)	
12					Midnight Special (to: 2:30, Fri) (cont.)	
1/79						
2						
3						
4						
5						
6						
7						
8						
9						
10						
11						
12						
1/80						
2						
3						
4						
5						
6						
7						
8						
9		Tonight Show Starring		Tomorrow Show (Mon-Thur)		
10		Johnny Carson		Midnight Special (Fri)		
11						
12						
1/81						
2						
3						
4						
5				Tomorrow Show (Mon-Thur)		
6				SCTV NETWORK 90 (Fri)		
7						

	11:00p.m.	11:30p.m.	12:00midnight	12:30a.m.	1:00a.m.	1:30a.m.
8		Tonight Show Starring		Tomorrow Show (Mon-Thur, cont.)		
9		Johnny Carson (cont.)		Sctv Network 90 (Fri, cont.)		

LATE NIGHT WITH DAVID LETTERMAN (Mon-Thur)
Sctv Network 90 (to: 2:00, Fri)

NBC NEWS OVERNIGHT (to: 2:30) (Mon-Thur)

Late Night With David Letterman (Mon-Thur)
FRIDAY NIGHT VIDEOS (to:2:00, Fri)

	11:00p.m.	11:30p.m.	12:00midnight	12:30a.m.	1:00a.m.	1:30a.m.
5		Tonight Show Starring		Late Night With David Letterman		
6		Johnny Carson (cont.)		(Mon-Thur, cont.) Friday Night Videos (to:2:00, Fri) (cont.)		
7						
8						
9						
10						
11						
12						
1/85						
2						
3						
4						
5						
6						
7						
8						
9						
10						
11						
12						
1/86						
2						
3						
4						
5						
6						
7						
8						
9						
10						
11						
12						
1/87						

	11:00p.m.	11:30p.m.	12:00midnight	12:30a.m.	1:00a.m.	1:30a.m.
2		Tonight Show Starring		Late Night With David Letterman		
3		Johnny Carson (cont.)		(Mon-Thur, cont.)		
				Friday Night Videos (to:2:00, Fri)		
4				(cont.)		
5						
6				Late Night With David Letterman		Friday Night
7						Videos (Fri)
						(to: 2:30)
8						
9						
10						
11						
12						
1/88						
2						
3						
4						
5						
6						
7						
8						LATER WITH BOB
9						COSTAS
						(Mon-Thur)
10						Friday Night
						Videos (Fri)
11						(to: 2:30)
12						
1/89						
2						
3						
4						
5						
6						
7						
8						

Late-Night NBC
Program Moves

Date	Time	Title (Minutes) — Type	Action	From/To
9/59	11:15	Jack Paar Show (105) — TK	x	
3/62	11:15	Jack Paar Show (105) — TK	c	
4/62	11:15	Tonight Show (105) — TK	d	
9/62	11:15	Tonight Show (105) — TK	c	
10/62	11:15	Tonight Show Starring Johnny Carson (105) — TK	d	
12/66	11:15	Tonight Show Starring Johnny Carson (105) — TK	m	To:11:30
1/67	11:30	Tonight Show Starring Johnny Carson (90) — TK	m	Fr:11:15
2/73	1:00	Midnight Special (90, f) — MU	d	
10/73	1:00	Tomorrow Show (60, m-r) — TK	d	
9/80	11:30	Tonight Show Starring Johnny Carson (90) — TK	m	To:11:30(60min)
9/80	1:00	Tomorrow Show (60, m-r) — TK	m	To:12:30
9/80	1:00	Midnight Special (90, f) — MU	m	To:12:30
9/80	11:30	Tonight Show Starring Johnny Carson (60) — TK	m#	Fr:11:30(90min)
9/80	12:30	Tomorrow Show (90, m-r) — TK	m	Fr:1
9/80	12:30	Midnight Special (90, f) — MU	m	Fr:1
5/81	12:30	Midnight Special (90, f) — MU	c	
5/81	12:30	SCTV Network 90 (90, f) — CY	d	
1/82	12:30	Tomorrow Show (90, m-r) — TK	c	
2/82	12:30	Late Night with David Letterman (60, m-r) — TK	d	
7/82	1:30	NBC News Overnight (60, m-r) — NW	d	
6/83	12:30	SCTV Network 90 (90, f) — CY	c	
7/83	12:30	Friday Night Videos (90, f) — MU	d	
12/83	1:30	NBC News Overnight (60, m-r) — NW	c	
5/87	12:30	Late Night with David Letterman (60, m-r) — TK	m	To:12:30(m-f)
5/87	12:30	Friday Night Videos (90, f) — MU	m	To:1:30(f)

Date	Time	Title (Minutes) — Type	Action	From/To
6/87	12:30	Late Night with David Letterman (60) — TK	m#	Fr:12:30(m-r)
6/87	1:30	Friday Night Videos (60, f) — MU	m#	Fr:12:30(f)
8/88	1:30	Later with Bob Costas (m-r) — IV	d#	

Late-Night NBC
Programming Moves Summary

1959–60

Key Programming Moves: NBC continued to air THE JACK PAAR SHOW in the 11:15 p.m.–1:00 a.m. time slot. This talk program was developed by Sylvester "Pat" Weaver, who also developed NBC's TODAY SHOW. Hugh Downs served as Jack Paar's sidekick and announcer, and Jose Melis was the program's bandleader. On Monday nights, a guest host was used, and on Friday nights, a rerun was shown.

1961–62

Series Premieres: The Tonight Show. *Key Programming Moves:* In March, Jack Paar left NBC's late-night program, and for the remainder of the season the program was simply called THE TONIGHT SHOW. A variety of guest hosts were employed for the remainder of the season. Hugh Downs stayed with the program as the announcer and sidekick until the end of the season. Skitch Henderson replaced Melis as the bandleader.

1962–63

Series Premieres: The Tonight Show Starring Johnny Carson. *Key Programming Moves:* Johnny Carson was brought in to be the new host of NBC's late-night program, now titled THE TONIGHT SHOW STARRING JOHNNY CARSON. Ed McMahon, Carson's longtime sidekick on the daytime quiz show WHO DO YOU TRUST, replaced Hugh Downs as the late-night show's announcer and host's sidekick. Skitch Henderson continued as the new show's bandleader.

244 / *Late-Night NBC Programming Moves Summary*

1964–65

Key Programming Moves: For the first time, NBC and Johnny Carson were challenged in the late-night time period. ABC'S NIGHTLIFE made its debut in November. It was not able to compete successfully against Carson, whose position as #1 in late-night was now beginning to take a firm hold.

1965–66

Key Programming Moves: Skitch Henderson left TONIGHT at the end of the season.

1966–67

Key Programming Moves: Milton DeLugg was appointed bandleader of THE TONIGHT SHOW STARRING JOHNNY CARSON, replacing Skitch Henderson. In January, THE CARSON SHOW was cut back from 105 minutes to 90 minutes. At the end of the season, DeLugg was replaced as bandleader.

1967–68

Key Programming Moves: Bandleader Doc Severinson joined the cast of THE TONIGHT SHOW STARRING JOHNNY CARSON. After facing a second challenge from ABC (THE JOEY BISHOP SHOW) which hurt CARSON's ratings in the beginning, THE TONIGHT SHOW's ratings kept improving during the 1967-68 season, maintaining NBC's dominant position in late-night.

1968–69

Key Programming Moves: THE TONIGHT SHOW STARRING JOHNNY CARSON continued to be the dominant program on television in late-night.

1969–70

Key Programming Moves: In spite of two new challenges (ABC's THE DICK CAVETT SHOW and CBS' THE MERV GRIFFIN SHOW), THE TONIGHT SHOW STARRING JOHNNY CARSON continued to be the number one rated late-night program on television. The 1969–70 season also became notable due to the TONIGHT SHOW's live presentation of Tiny Tim's wedding.

1972–73

Series Premieres: The Midnight Special. *Key Programming Moves:* Production of THE TONIGHT SHOW STARRING JOHNNY CARSON was moved from New York City to Los Angeles. In February, NBC introduced THE MIDNIGHT SPECIAL; airing on Fridays from 1–2:30 a.m., this program featured contemporary pop and rock music artists.

1973–74

Series Premieres: The Tomorrow Show. *Key Programming Moves:* NBC introduced THE TOMORROW SHOW, a 60 minute talk/interview program hosted by Tom Snyder. It was scheduled in the time slot following THE TONIGHT SHOW STARRING JOHNNY CARSON on Monday through Thursday. THE MIDNIGHT SPECIAL continued to air in the slot following TONIGHT on Friday.

1974–75

Key Programming Moves: In December, production of THE TOMORROW SHOW was moved from Los Angeles to New York City.

1976–77

Key Programming Moves: In June, production of THE TOMORROW SHOW returned to Los Angeles from New York City.

1979–80

Key Programming Moves: Production of THE TOMORROW SHOW moved back to New York City at the start of the season.

1980–81

Series Premieres: SCTV Network 90. *Key Programming Moves:* THE TONIGHT SHOW STARRING JOHNNY CARSON was cut back to 60 minutes, airing 11:30 p.m.–12:30 a.m., and THE TOMORROW SHOW was expanded to 90 minutes, airing 12:30–2 a.m., Monday through Thursday. THE MID-NIGHT SPECIAL aired in the 12:30–2 a.m. slot on Friday. Rona Barrett was added to the cast of THE TOMORROW SHOW at the beginning of the season. She left the program in April, leaving Tom Snyder as the sole host. In May, NBC cancelled THE MIDNIGHT SPECIAL and replaced it with SCTV NET-WORK 90, a 90 minute comedy-variety series airing on Friday, following TONIGHT.

1981–82

Series Premieres: Late Night with David Letterman; NBC News Over-night. *Key Programming Moves:* THE TOMORROW SHOW was cancelled in January. NBC replaced it with a new 60 minute talk program aimed at a younger audience, titled LATE NIGHT WITH DAVID LETTERMAN. LETTER-MAN aired Monday through Thursday in the 12:30–1:30 a.m. slot. SCTV NETWORK 90 continued to air on Friday in the 12:30–2 a.m. slot. In July, NBC introduced NBC NEWS OVERNIGHT, a one-hour news analysis pro-gram, airing Monday through Thursday from 1:30–2:30 a.m.

1982–83

Series Premieres: Friday Night Videos. *Key Programming Moves:* NBC cancelled SCTV NETWORK 90 in June and replaced it with FRIDAY NIGHT VIDEOS, a 90 minute collection of music videos hosted by a different personality each week.

1983–84

Key Programming Moves: NBC NEWS OVERNIGHT was cancelled in December.

1986–87

Key Programming Moves: In June, LATE NIGHT WITH DAVID LET-TERMAN began airing five nights a week. FRIDAY NIGHT VIDEOS was cut back to 60 minutes and moved into the 1:30–2:30 a.m. slot on Fridays.

1988–89

Series Premieres: Later with Bob Costas. *Key Programming Moves:* NBC introduced LATER WITH BOB COSTAS, a 30 minute interview program scheduled after LATE NIGHT WITH DAVID LETTERMAN on Monday through Thursday. It managed to capture a small but loyal audience, and at season's end, the outlook was promising.

Fox Late-Night

October 1986–August 1989

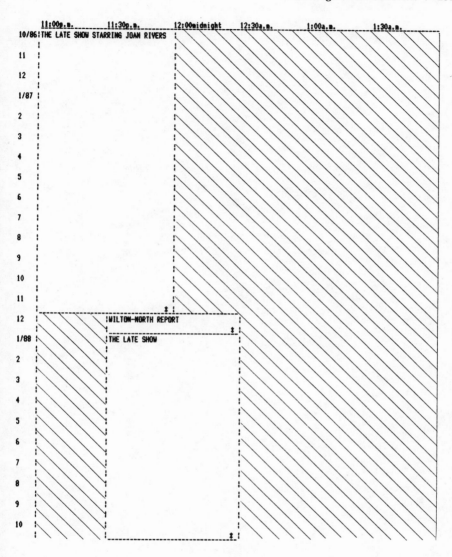

	11:00p.m.	11:30p.m.	12:00midnight	12:30a.m.	1:00a.m.	1:30a.m.

10/86 THE LATE SHOW STARRING JOAN RIVERS

11

12

1/87

2

3

4

5

6

7

8

9

10

11

12 WILTON-NORTH REPORT

1/88 THE LATE SHOW

2

3

4

5

6

7

8

9

10

Late-Night Fox
Program Moves

Date	Time	Title (Minutes)—Type	Action	From/To
10/86	11:00	The Late Show Starring Joan Rivers —(60)—TK	d	
11/87	11:00	The Late Show Starring Joan Rivers —(60)—TK	c	
12/87	11:30	The Wilton-North Report (60)—CY	d	
12/87	11:30	The Wilton-North Report (60)—CY	c	
1/88	11:30	The Late Show (60)—TK	d	
10/88	11:30	The Late Show (60)—TK	c	

Late-Night Fox
Programming Moves Summary

1986–87

Series Premieres: The Late Show Starring Joan Rivers. *Key Programming Moves:* The Fox Broadcasting Company entered the late-night arena in October with a 60 minute late-night talk show, THE LATE SHOW STARRING JOAN RIVERS. The program started out promising, but, as the season went on, the ratings slowly but steadily declined, and by season's end the series was in trouble.

1987–88

Series Premieres: The Late Show; The Wilton-North Report. *Key Programming Moves:* Due to declining ratings, THE LATE SHOW STARRING JOAN RIVERS was finally cancelled in November. Following the cancellation of Ms. Rivers' program, Fox introduced THE WILTON-NORTH REPORT, which lasted only one month. In January, Fox introduced a redesigned late-night talk show, titled simply THE LATE SHOW. Using a variety of rotating hosts, this program never really caught on and was cancelled less than one year after its debut.

Index

Entries in **boldface** refer to individuals. All other entries are to shows.